D0904890

PEFFERLAW PUBLIC LIBRARY   DATE RECEIVED

331   Hiley, Michael.   DEC 1 6 1980
.40941   Victorian working women; portraits from
Hil   life. Boston, D. R. Godine, 1980[1979]
              142 p. ill., ports.
              Includes bibliographical references.

           1. Women - Employment - Great Britain -
           History. I. Title.
           0879233249   1014943 LC

CHECKED FEB 1 9 1985

48/Pe

Victorian Working Women: Portraits from Life

Michael Hiley

VICTORIAN WORKING WOMEN:
Portraits from Life

David R. Godine, Publisher   Boston

First U.S. edition published in 1980 by
David R. Godine, Publisher, Inc.
306 Dartmouth Street
Boston, Massachusetts 02116

Copyright © 1979 by Michael Hiley

All rights reserved. No part of this book
may be used or reproduced in any manner
whatsoever without written permission except
in the case of brief quotations embodied
in critical articles and reviews.

First published in 1979 by The Gordon Fraser Gallery Ltd.,
London and Bedford

LIBRARY OF CONGRESS CATALOGING IN PUBLICATION DATA

Hiley, Michael.
    Victorian working women.

    Includes bibliographical references and index.
    1. Women – Employment – Great Britain – History.
I. Title.
HD6135.H54   1980   331.4′0941   79-92110

ISBN 0-87923-324-9

Design & Typography by Peter Guy
Printed and bound by Halliday Lithograph Corporation
MANUFACTURED IN THE UNITED STATES OF AMERICA

FOR
MARIE HILEY

PEFFERLAW PUBLIC LIBRARY

Contents

Acknowledgements

The main source of the documents quoted, and the photographs reproduced in this book is the Munby collection in the Library of Trinity College, Cambridge. I am grateful to the Master and Fellows of Trinity College for permission to use this material, and to Dr. Philip Gaskell, the Librarian, and his staff for all the help they have given me over the past four years.

I am also grateful to Leicester Polytechnic for the support given to my research, and would like to thank David Bethel, the Director, and Dr. Sydney Cotson, Deputy Director and Chairman of the Research Committee.

My thanks also to Madeleine Ginsberg, of the Victoria and Albert Museum, who drew my attention to the album of *cartes-de-visite* of mine tip girls in the Gallery of English Costume at Manchester; to Andrew Lanyon for information on the photographs of Lewis Harding; and to Doug Gray for information on the history of the mining industry.

My research was made easier by the help given by the staff of many libraries, especially those of Cambridge University Library and Leicester University Library. In preparing this book for publication I count myself lucky to have both as editors and as friends Peter Guy and James Fraser, whose advice has been invaluable.

The Munby documents at Trinity College run into millions of words, and in reading these I have realised just how painstaking a job was done by Derek Hudson in producing his book *Munby, Man of Two Worlds; The Life and Diaries of Arthur J. Munby, 1828–1910* (London 1972). Both of us have had to make selections from the vast amount of written material available. To complement my selection of extracts which relate particularly to working women, his book provides more detailed information on other aspects of Munby's life.

Further information on pit brow women can be found in Angela John's forthcoming book *By the Sweat of their Brow: Women Workers at Victorian Coal Mines*. Peter Frank is investigating the work of Yorkshire fisherwomen – see his article 'Women's Work in the Yorkshire Inshore Fishing Industry' in *Oral History* for Spring 1976.

All the photographs, sketches and illustrations are from the Munby collection at Trinity College, except those below, which are reproduced by courtesy of the following institutions:

Pages 10, 33, 61, 73 (left), 74, 83, & 87 Public Record Office.

Pages 13, 22, 46, 66, & 70 (below) the Syndics of Cambridge University Library.

Pages 23, 25, 26 (right), 37, 39 (both), 60, & 79 Leicester University Library.

Page 45 by permission of the British Library.

Page 49 (all) Birmingham Public Libraries.

Pages 55 (and title page) & 57 Birmingham Public Libraries (Local Studies Department).

Page 69 Gernsheim Collection, Humanities Research Center, The University of Texas at Austin.

Page 71 (right) Victoria and Albert Museum.

Page 71 (left) Royal Archives, Windsor Castle. Reproduced by gracious permission of Her Majesty the Queen.

Page 73 (right) Royal Institution of Cornwall.

Page 76 (all) Sandwell Public Libraries.

Pages 96, 97 (all), 98 (both), & 130 City of Manchester Art Galleries.

I am grateful to Faber and Faber Ltd. for permission to quote from Gwen Raverat's book *Period Piece: A Cambridge Childhood*.

Michael Hiley. Leicester, June 1979

I: VICTORIAN WORKING WOMEN

South West Lancashire
Pit Brow Woman, 1886
(possibly Elizabeth Halliwell
of Blundell's Pemberton
Colliery).
By Herbert Wragg of Wigan.

1: Working Women

'If I had the means, I would investigate, being now old enough to do so without misconstruction, the moral and physical statistics of labouring women all over the world.'

Arthur Munby writing in his diary, 1859.

FROM the shadows under the northern span of London Bridge a girl emerged, carrying on her head an immense load of sacking. She toiled up the steps to reach the level of the bridge and, on reaching the top, threw down her load on to the parapet and leaned against the wall to rest, before crossing the bridge to her home in Bermondsey. It was going to be a warm afternoon – the showers were clearing and there was a thunderstorm somewhere away over north London. She was making her way back from the warehouses near Billingsgate, and had the oily yellow hands which marked her out as a sackmaker. People crossing the bridge did not give her a second glance as she stood trying to catch her breath and rolling her shoulders in an attempt to ease the ache in her muscles. Bermondsey sackwomen were an everyday sight around there. After a few minutes rest, she pulled the burden off the parapet, hoisted it back on to her head and continued her journey over the bridge, completely unaware that, a few yards below her on a landing stage at the edge of the river, a man had been watching every move she made.

Arthur Munby was waiting at London Bridge for a boat to take him back up the Thames to Whitehall, where he worked in the office of the Ecclesiastical Commissioners. He happened to see the girl as she started up the steps; his interest for the next few minutes was exclusively on her, and his observations formed the main part of his diary entry for that day, Wednesday 5 June 1861:

Her head of course was bare: her hair had been drawn tight behind her ears and knotted behind, but was now all rough and rumpled and adust, with carrying the sacks. She wore an old gown of nameless material, sodden with laborious sweat; her broad breast (for she was a tall, strongly built wench of twenty or so) was loosely covered with a red and orange kerchief, the two ends hanging in a knot; a tattered blue and white apron hung from her wide waist, and her gown, gathered up under it, showed beneath a short and very ragged petticoat, below which were a pair of strong ankles and large feet, clad in dirty white stockings and muddy masculine boots, worn and shapeless. A coarse plaid shawl fell back from her square shoulders, as she stood against the wall, her feet planted wide apart on the pavement, and one stout but pallid arm akimbo, and the other resting with its wrist upon her hip, the large bony hand, yellowed with grease and oil, falling free in a clumsy ease. So she stood; now rolling from side to side, now hitching up her shoulders, now rubbing the back of her hand across her nose or mouth: every action and posture rude and ungainly, but full of loose and supple strength. Her head drooped forward; and her young but bony face, with its listless eyes and wide open mouth, had a dull weary stolid look, like that of a carthorse in the traces. I stood looking at her several minutes; and the crowd of men and of welldressed or working women swept past her always; but there she remained, as careless of her own appearance, as unconscious of all around her, as that same cart horse waiting at a door.

At last she lifted her arms, and pulled down from the wall upon her head the long mass of empty sacks bound into one with ropes. Her face was half buried in the burden, which was much wider than her broad shoulders: she stood up strongly under it, and strode away into the throng.

So much for that sight.[1]

That is all there is to it. An unknown sackmaker crosses London Bridge, completely unaware that she has been the centre of attention of a man standing at the water's edge. Munby is pleased to have seen her, describing her as 'an unusually fine one', and it is clear that he must have seen many such women sackmakers. He writes of her as if she has been collected – a specimen to be pinned to a board in order to be compared with others of similar species. Certainly he has noticed the most minute details – she was wearing not just a kerchief, but *a red and orange kerchief, the two ends hanging in a knot*; she wears *white* stockings and *masculine* boots which are *muddy, worn and shapeless*. He is building up a very clear and specific image of a particular woman. Every movement she makes is recorded, as she stands *now rolling from side to side, now hitching up her shoulders, now rubbing the back of her hand across her nose or mouth*. He admires her sheer strength and uses an extraordinary simile to describe her dull, weary, stolid look – *like that of a carthorse in the traces*.

Why is he writing all this down? What purpose is there in this obsessive recording of minor details? Why single her out from the crowd at all? He doesn't seem to be amassing material for a social history – his description tells us a great deal about one individual sackmaker, but almost nothing about the business of making sacks. His interest is in the fact that the sackmaker is a woman – a woman of the working classes going about the hard business of earning her living by sheer physical effort.

Munby classifies her and yet describes her in such a way that she remains an individual. She is not necessarily a representative sackmaker, but then neither is she only a picturesque vignette of the hardworking poor glimpsed in passing. For Munby this is not merely a random encounter devoid of meaning. It joins all the other hundreds of encounters from which he has created a pantheon in diary form to those working women whom he finds worthy of praise. He is interested especially in women engaged in hard physical labour. He finds tall, strong, working women admirable; he takes a great interest in their horny hands, hardened and calloused with labour. One senses that his interest in these horny-handed daughters of toil grew rapidly into an obsession – an obsession for which we should be grateful, because the energy with which he tackles his self-appointed rôle as investigator of working women produces the enormous volume of diary descriptions, and prompts him to build up the collection of photographs of working women upon which this book is based.

Munby lived in the heart of London and was the tenant of 6 Fig Tree Court, Inner Temple from 1857 to his death in 1910. He was close enough to the centre of the city to make most journeys on foot and he took a delight in walking and observing women in the streets, speaking to them whenever an opportunity presented itself or could with decency be engineered. He knew the best places from which to observe the passing crowd: 'London Bridge, more than any place I know here, seems to be the great thoroughfare for young working women and girls. One meets them at every step: young women carrying wooden cages full of hats, which yet want the silk and the binding; costergirls, often dirty and sordid, going to fill their empty baskets; and above all, female sackmakers.'[2] The bridge carried very heavy traffic. In 1859 the Commissioner of City Police arranged for a count to be made of people and vehicles crossing the bridge and found that during one period of twenty-four hours, 4,483 cabs, 4,286 omnibuses, 9,245 waggons and carts, and 2,430 other vehicles crossed the bridge. They carried 60,836 persons, and a further 107,074 people crossed the bridge on foot. George du Maurier's illustration *The Living Stream at London Bridge – On the Bridge* gives some idea of the throng of Londoners who presented themselves to such an observant onlooker as Munby – or, indeed, du Maurier.[3]

George du Maurier, *The Living Stream at London Bridge – On the Bridge*. Illustration from *London Society*, 1863.

Arthur Munby would not have been particularly interested in the never-ending traffic clattering by, nor would he have cast more than a passing glance at the businessmen and clerks on their way to their offices, warehouses and workshops. Like the man with the monocle and the boy eating the apple, his eye would have been drawn immediately to the girl in the cloak. His observation of working women in London over the years would have enabled him to make an informed guess at her occupation – sifting the clues given by her cloak, her bonnet, her hairstyle, her bearing, the fact that she was alone, and the fact that she had to suffer the ogling stares of passers-by. He would probably have placed her in what he called 'the milliner class', and – given some suitable pretext – would have gone on to interview the young lady.

Here is a typical chance meeting which took place when Munby was crossing Westminster Bridge:

I passed a girl whom it was not easy to classify. She wore a net for her hair, a very shabby but once fashionable bonnet, a grey shawl stained and worn, a lilac cotton frock and apron, and stout laced boots. A strong sturdy creature, with a richbrown skin to her comely honest face; her hands too were large and brown, and she did not try to hide them.

A strange cross between a milliner and a field-wench: she must be a mechanic of some kind. I went up to her: 'May I ask, what is your trade?' 'I'm a brush-drawer by trade, Sir,' said the girl, frankly: 'but I work at a laundry now; what with the machines, a respectable girl cant get a living at the brush-drawing: I used to earn 12 or 14 shillings a week at it, and now I can only get 7 or 8. But I earn 2/6 a day at ironing, and 2/ at washing.'

A remarkably healthy and robust girl she was: only seventeen, she said, but she looked twenty: lives in Horsemonger Lane, and her name – Louisa Stapleton![4]

The encounter is over. The working girl with the distinguished name goes on her way, Munby's curiosity has been satisfied, and the details of the meeting will later be entered in his diary. While she is perhaps still wondering why he should want to speak to her, he is already off on the omnibus to a luncheon appointment in Clapham, noticing that at all the houses along his route Saturday cleaning is going on: 'I counted twenty maid servants at work out of doors, mostly on their knees.'

His concern with working women was energetic and obsessive. Lewis Carroll (the Rev. C. L. Dodgson) revealed a great deal about his own preoccupations in his remark 'I am fond of children, except boys'. Arthur Munby was fond of working people, except men.

This rather strait-laced civil servant was eventually to become a champion of the rights of working women, from motives which were so private and deeply rooted in his character that he would probably have found it difficult to put into words his reasons for searching out working women wherever he travelled. In 1886 he wrote that 'for reasons of my own, I have for more than thirty years studied the subject of female labour, not merely in books and at second hand, but with my own eyes and on the spot.'[5] He was so enamoured of his self-imposed task of social observation that as early as 1859 he confided to his diary: 'If I had the means, I would investigate being now old enough to do so without misconstruction [he was now thirty], the moral and physical statistics of labouring women all over the world.'[6]

Munby was always interested when he found a new business in which women were engaged. He discovered 'a new form of female labour' one evening whilst out looking for women working in the market gardens in south London:

In the fork of the two railways, in a road just beyond the buildings and near Blue Anchor lane, a dreary lonely way, I met a very strange looking girl, without a bonnet or a shawl, wearing a soiled ragged gown, and boots to match; having her arms bare, and her throat wrapped up in flannel; for she was very hoarse.

A tall hulking wench of eighteen, rolling along like a sailor; but with a simple and modest countenance.

Considering her in vain, I asked her if she worked in the market gardens. No, she did not, she answered civilly. Then, said I, what is your trade? 'Sir,' she meekly replied, looking me straight in the face, 'I *scrapes trotters.*' The answer was so comic and the speaker so serious, that I hardly forbore to laugh: but perceiving that this was a 'find', I went on to ask particulars. The trotterscraping institution was close by, and full in sight: a group of low wooden buildings, standing suspiciously alone in the field. And straightway a second girl, of the same age, came out of it and joined us. . . . I learnt from her (and afterwards from the tollkeeper near) that these Works are Glue, Offal, Bone, works, and belong to a Mr. Brier or Bryant; and that forty or fifty girls and women are employed there. 'We scrapes' said this belle of the Boneworks, not only trotters, but also 'bullocks' feet, Sir, and horses' feet. We scrapes the hair off 'em, and steeps 'em in lime, and prepares the hoofs.'. . .

Now, can anyone imagine an occupation more loathsome, more certain (one would think) to coarsen and unsex a young woman and destroy all grace of form and character, than to sit among heaps of offal all day, and scrape and clean the gory and half-putrid feet that are cut from carcases of sheep and horses and bullocks? Yet these two girls, who do this daily, were not gross nor unsexed: *they* did not grin or giggle or stare impudently at the stranger, or make ribald innuendoes one of another, as sewing girls and suchlike often do: on the contrary, they were thoroughly respectable and respectful in behaviour; and one of them, at least, was brisk and clear-headed, and equal to any country girl for beauty.[7]

One can begin to recognise the distinctive mixture which goes to make up Munby's diary entries on working women. They are not written for publication, and so he makes no pretence of standing back to provide an objective analysis of the work and wages of these trotterscrapers. His description of the meeting reveals his interest in their appearance – an interest which does not blind him to the fact that although the second girl looked 'most forlorn and repulsive' in her ragged clothes, she was 'a stout buxom lass, rosy and healthy' whom he is pleased to talk with. His ear for dialogue is acute; he asks 'And is it nice work?' and she replies 'Well Sir, it's nice for them as likes it'.

Is it possible that Munby may have seen himself as the bold knight braving the unknown to rescue (in this particular adventure) 'the belle of the Boneworks' from the glutinous grasp of the king of the offal factory? Certainly there was a part of him ready to play the role of the conventional middle-class male in order to register surprise, if not shock, that women should have to work at such hard, stomach-churning tasks. But his mission was to observe and not to reform. Indeed, he would have had no wish to take these girls away from their work, provided they were happy to do it.

The dramatic content of the meeting on the lonely road between the fork in the railways is heightened not only by Munby's personal observations, but also by the fact that he does not exclude himself from the meeting by editing what was said to produce a monologue of verbatim evidence. He is certainly interested in the details of the job the girls do; he draws out the fact that they are paid only two shillings a week – a starvation wage – and verifies this from the second girl out of hearing of the other. But his ambition to investigate 'the moral and physical statistics of labouring women' produces both hard fact and personal comment. Does scraping rotting flesh off bones 'unsex' a girl? Did the girls behave 'impudently' or stare at the stranger – were they respectful to this inquisitive middle-class gentleman? Munby both poses and answers his own questions, usually to his own satisfaction if not always to ours. The question of what work is suitable for women is raised at once, and this, together with his sensitivity to what most contemporary observers would have considered the dangers of the women being 'coarsened', 'unsexed' and 'degraded' by such work is an ever-present concern in Munby's writings on working women.

He never organised his extensive information on female labour for publication. There were moments when it seemed possible that he would be able to merge his driving interest with earning a living. For example, in 1866 he went to the Civil Service Commission to enquire about the post of Factory Inspector, but was disappointed to find that the salary was only £300 a year. In 1863 he had travelled on his own initiative to Northumberland to investigate the 'Bondagers' – 'so called female serfs' who worked in the fields. He produced for himself a brief report which he entered in his diary, setting down his findings under various headings: Area of Employment, Sex and Age, Hiring and Wages, Kinds of Work, Times of Appearing, Numbers, Dress, Education, and general comments. Probably no one but Munby read it – a private report on a private interest. It is sad to read a diary entry dating from six years later:

Went to Hansard's in Abingdon Street about 5 p.m., and spent an hour there, studying the evidence in the First Report of the 1867 Commission on Employment of 'Children and Women' (save the mark!) in Agriculture. Would that I had been one of these Commissioners! But the Northumberland Comr., Mr. Henley, does full justice to those splendid lasses, the Bondagers. It is a comfort to me also, sitting here fastbound, to know that women so vigorous and so picturesque exist, and are at work, though far away.[8]

Munby might have found difficulty in repressing his bubbling enthusiasm for such 'splendid lasses', but it is a pity that he could find no channel for his energies and spent his life in a job which hardly began to draw on his real abilities. He became a self-appointed Commissioner, travelling the country on his mission, and it must have pleased him that the Wigan pit girls came to give him the nickname 'The Inspector'.

His enquiries were shaped by personal preference and by force of circumstance, and many women workers – for example needlewomen and factory girls – interested him hardly at all. The evidence to be gleaned from his diaries is, therefore, fragmentary and inconclusive, except in the case of the Lancashire pit brow lasses, where he provides extensive information. The scenes he witnesses are usually happened upon by chance, and he provides us with vivid descriptions of sights and events which would be beneath the dignity of most passers-by to acknowledge, let alone show interest in.

Henry Mayhew's monumental study of street life in London, *London Labour and the London Poor* (1851/62),* had brought in its wake a generation of popular social reporters who, in the 1860s and 1870s, searched out scenes of 'low life' and provided vignettes of the life of the poor. They brought back exciting reports from the slums into which their middle-class readership rarely dared venture. Their reports read like despatches from a distant and barbarous land, where the likes of trotterscraping were routine occupations. In 1851 Mayhew had promised his readers 'information concerning a large body of persons' of whom the public had 'less knowledge than of the most distant tribes of the earth'. Twenty-five years later, James Greenwood reported on 'Curiosities of "Alley Life"' in a book which he titled *Low-Life Deeps: An Account of the Strange Fish to be Found There*. Spitalfields provided him with very odd fish to be netted:

Strange trades are carried on in these slums, and occupations are followed which in civilised parts are never dreamt of, except it be in exceptionally bad dreams. One does not like even to hint at the way in which scores of poor wretches in the locality pick up a living, nor would I myself have believed it had I not been told it as a fact, by a gentleman whose veracity is unimpeachable. There is an awful little alley, for instance, in the neighbourhood of Hales's tallow factory, consisting of about twenty houses, inhabited almost entirely by folk who collect the ordure of dogs, which is used for tanning purposes. I say that the alley in question is occupied almost entirely by this class, and, repulsive as the trade is, it is preferable to that of the dreadful exceptions. There are but few left there now, I am informed, but not very long since the residents of this delectable spot consisted chiefly of 'cat-flayers' – whose sole means of living was to go out at night with their sacks and sticks, hunting for cats to be slaughtered for the sake of their skins. . . . It is unfortunate . . . that to be saleable the hide must be taken from the body of the animal while it is still in existence, and still more so that the villainous cat-flayers are not deterred by this difficulty.[9]

*Mayhew's original intention was to produce a series of volumes which would form 'a cyclopaedia of the industry, the want, and the vice of the great Metropolis'.

You can almost hear the shocked intake of breath as the reader reaches the end of the chapter, sets aside the book, and rings for tea.

Munby would not have been interested in such sensational reporting. When he wanted information on working women he turned to Government reports and census tables. To flesh out the dry bones of statistics, everyday life provided him with first-hand experience of how others lived; here he witnesses a dramatic event after midnight one Saturday on his way home from a party:

She was a prostitute, in Regent Street; an elegantly drest girl of twenty or so. Just before I came up, I saw her reel, and then sink down helpless into the gutter. A young man who was before me rushed on and lifted her up and set her against a post and stayed her with his arm round her waist; a dirty woman – the only one present – refused to stay; but several young clerks and suchlike, gathered about, and tried to rouse her. She, with her fashionable clothes bedraggled and her young girlish face besotted with drink, stood motionless, staring with glassy eyes, while her head fell heavily from side to side, as she tried to clutch at the men round her, and stuttered out her professional formula 'Comehomewishmemydear.' Meanwhile, the young men patted her on the cheek or chucked her under the chin; and he who held her (a Yankee he seemed to be) made fun for the others by affecting to dispose of her person. 'Come', he cried 'you shall have her for nothing tonight! Here's a bargain – this fine young woman going for nothing!' And the rest laughed and jested accordingly. At length the wretched girl blurted out 'Soho Square' when they asked where she lived. A passing hansom stopped; and, after falling under the wheel into the gutter again, she was thrust in, and sank a dead heap on the floor of the cab; believing all the while that one of the men was going with her home. The man drove away; and as soon as all was over, the policeman for whom I had waited so long came up.

What a subject! Childhood, and girlhood, and then – *this*.[10]

Munby was a great listener and, on the occasions when he had prompted a woman to pour out her troubles to him, he could reproduce her torrent of words in his diary complete with phrasing, stresses and mispronunciations. One Saturday afternoon in Park Lane he saw a young woman dressed in tattered and once-fashionable clothes and stopped her 'because she looked forlorn and was going about with a bit of paper, asking the way, and evidently in earnest':

Yes, it was *him* she was a looking for: him, the faithless one, lately prentice opposite our master's war'us but now Policeman (which his number's 14 Sir I've just got it given) and on his beat in South Audley Street. *Where* is South Audley Street? That is the question: and oh, *wont* I fly at him when I do set eyes on him, that's all! The old story: not so much seduction, as willing concubinage. Two children: he took a room for us and I've lived with him two years, but not married more's the pity; and one [is] dead, . . . and there's one boy left and the Superintendent as I see him just now at *Wine* Street and told him all *that* I did Well Sir he says let him have the child he says and make him keep it – keep it? he *shall* but I'm blest if I'll part with my child for no one and I wish I was dead and the child too and then there'd be an end to us both!

The girl had been brought up, she said, to

work in a pickle warehouse: but since he deserted her she had gone into casual service, . . . 'and not a penny will he give me for the child! Why, I met him on London Bridge the other morning and I says Bill I says I've no money give me a halfpenny for the steamer, cos I thought he'd be shamed not for to give me no more, and he just took and chucked me a halfpenny as if I was a beggar, I aint got no more, he says, and him with 18/ a week but I'll get him turned out of the force that I will if he won't do nothin' for the child! And there's my clothes in pawn that I'm not decent to go to place, and me sittin' like pillgarlick in a corner, and all for him!' *Pillgarlick in a corner*: why that phrase alone is worth half an hour's detention.[11]

Munby maintains his distance. She uses a phrase which interests him, but she speaks 'vile Cockney' and he feels little sympathy for her plight: 'Love? who speaks of it among such folk? It was a passing fancy, she confessed, and she cared for him no longer.'

But this graduate of Trinity College, Cambridge, this trained barrister, friend of Rossetti and Ruskin, had a compassion for working women which was extraordinary for a man of his class. He had not hardened his heart to the feelings of those women whose rank in society and station in life enabled others to treat them as worthless pawns in a game. He felt especial sympathy for those whose sex and status laid them most open to abuse, for example the servant girls employed in the all-male London Clubs:

Dined at the University Club. In the smoking room after dinner, as I was quietly reading Froude* over a pipe, comes a phenomenon: a young Guardsman, full of airy speeches, who frankly tells the company how So and So of this Club has done a thing for which one must 'chaff' him; has, in fact, seduced or tried to seduce a 'fishmaid belonging to the Club' You observe – 'a *fishmaid*'; simply a nameless creature of that contemptible species; a female animal unknown to us, abiding somewhere underground. And, as if to point the moral, when I left the smokingroom I met on the backstairs one of these very creatures; scullion or the like, coming up from kitchenwork. Human, she seemed: looked like a maid of eighteen, with meek face, drest in servile cap and apron and sleeveless cotton frock. Seeing me, one of her many masters, she stopped, and humbly drew back into a corner, with her bare arms against the wall, to let my worship pass. And my worship passed without deigning to look at her.[12]

To have offered to let her go first was unthinkable; to look her in the eye might be misinterpreted.

Over the years it was inevitable that his motives in accosting women would be misinterpreted, and in his time Munby was thought by various ignorant people to be the Fenian, 'Colonel' Kelly, and, late in life, Jack the Ripper. He seemed to be blissfully unaware of the compromising situations in which he constantly placed himself. Recognising him for the true innocent that he was, Fate always arranged a suitable escape. On one occasion he was just beginning to discuss the finer points of cornet playing with a girl performing

*J. A. Froude (1818–1894), the historian and biographer; he was an acquaintance of Munby.

for a crowd in King Street when his friend Walter Severn came along by chance. Munby's reaction to the scene had been 'How interesting'. Severn's was quite different: 'How odd! . . . what audacity!' and, 'fearful of the listening folk', he hurried Munby away. Munby complained in his diary that 'the trumpeted girl remains a mystery'.[13]

In June 1864 he watched a performance of nigger minstrels in the street. Two girls made up with lampblack were accompanied by two men whom he described as '"cads" of the lowest type':

As their hearers consisted of a crowd of street boys and girls, a few working men and women, a soldier or two, and myself, it was but natural that they should sing at me, in hope of getting repaid. So accordingly the fair negress presented herself before my lordship, curtsying and saying 'Please Sir!' and holding out her black hand and her tambourine, with a smile which even from the lampblacked lips could not but produce effect. . . . And now I turned to go away, for one of the men came up, importuning me as 'Captain' and 'Major' for another gift. But just as I was dismissing him, a female voice at my side cried out 'Táke that, for bothering the gentleman!' and a stout bare arm flashed across me and dealt the hapless nigger such a blow on the chest, that he fell backward against the wall. I looked round to see my champion, and beheld a tall strong Irish costergirl, who stood and stared contemptuously upon the man she had vanquished. 'Get along with your ugly mug!' exclaimed the indignant maiden; and he did: he slunk away without a word, afraid to face her fair fist again. Then she turned to me, her face crimson, her eyes still flashing; and before I had time to compliment her on her prowess 'did ye ever see the like o' that, Sir?' said she: meaning, not the vigour of her arm, as one might think, but the exhibition of 'Serenading' that we had just heard. 'To see them two girls' she went on 'standing in the street wid their faces blacked – it's shameful, *I* call it!' Well, said I, I dont know: why shouldn't it be as honest as crying oranges? '*We* dont cry oranges', she retorted: 'we're costermongers, and sells cabbages and that'. Yes, and you hawk them about the streets, dont you? 'Well Sir, and if I do, would I be after blacking me face like them two divels, think ye?'

She then gave her opinion that they were nothing better than streetwalkers doing this sort of thing for a change.[14]

How pleased Munby must have felt to have been 'rescued' by that Irish girl. To be rescued by a working man would have been embarrassing at best. But to find a heroine among working women and to have her take command of the situation was almost too much to hope for. Here were more strapping, self-reliant lasses to admire and to talk to. And off he strolled down the Strand through the fashionable crowd with the costergirl and her friend by his side – women who were not ashamed of their position in life, whose simple working dress emphasised the frivolous nonsense of the 'bloated crinolines' around them, and whose 'brown victorious arms' were a match for any man.

2: 'Suggestive Contrasts'

'A strong homely simple woman, going about the hard work of common life in the midst of idleness and luxury, is to me an object of the highest interest.'

Munby writing in his diary, 1862.

THE costergirls brushing past the crinolined ladies in the Strand would have provided Munby with what he called 'suggestive contrasts'; that is, contrasts between women from widely differing social backgrounds. It was by maintaining contact with both ends of the social scale that he was able to savour these contrasts and muse upon their implications. And it is his unusually extensive view of the social scene which makes his observations of particular interest a century later.

Three days before his encounter with the brush-drawer on Westminster Bridge, he had attended a dinner party in fashionable Montagu Square:

I took down to dinner a Miss Abercromby, a very loveable young creature, whose dress was charmingly original and picturesque. She wore a black velvet skirt, its folds defined by a line of white silk near the ground; a little Swiss boddice of the same, half concealed by a full shirt of pure white lawn, coming up to the throat; its sleeves puffed like those of Henry VIII's time, and bound with narrow fillets of black velvet. This, with a single blush rose in light brown hair, and with an exquisite figure, made her the observed of all the room in the evening.... My companion on the other side was Lady MacGregor ... Both Lady MacGregor and Miss Abercromby, in their several ways, as a matronly woman and a tender girl, were excellent examples of that best result of feminine training – a frankness and naïve gentleness which a village charmer could not surpass, clothed in such graceful ease and dignity of manner, as only educated society can give.[1]

At balls and dinner parties such as this, he was used to acting as escort to the 'sumptuous swanlike being' who was to partner him for the evening. He moved in such high social circles that the heiresses with whom he came into contact – heiresses who were being carefully chaperoned as they displayed themselves on the society circuit – had the most staggering 'price on their heads'. One evening he was told that 'there were two hundred-thousand-pounders in the room tonight,' but his response to such heiresses was, in society's eyes at least, perverse. 'Heiresses' he wrote 'somehow set me longing for a poor hardworking girl, their opposite – her coarse but genuine tints the complement of their splendid dyes.'[2]

The du Maurier illustration gives us a glimpse of fashionable society and the fragile creatures against which Munby could contrast his working women. The engraving was used to illustrate a magazine story[3] and was captioned 'I am spell-bound by the sight of Laura Matilda!' The young man stands transfixed by the sight of two young women – Laura Matilda is helping to button the glove of a friend who has been playing the piano for the assembled company. This was the world into which Munby had entry, and 'Laura Matilda' became one of his nicknames for the skilled exponents of what he called 'fineladyism'.

His attitude towards those who represented the upper crust of cosmopolitan life was ambivalent to say the least. He maintained his links with high society, he would have us believe, only in order to despise its false glitter and its pretensions. And yet he never saw himself as anything other than an educated middle-class gentleman who was – however unwillingly – a part of this world. At social gatherings he was no doubt his usual, meticulously polite self, but he could indicate his real feelings in his diary with a touch of irony: 'at 10.30 went to a party at the Ashursts', 7 Prince of Wales's Terrace, Kensington. More Sumptuous women, and music, and buzz of infinite chatter, and crushing and crowding, and joy of taking down Madame Chose, whom you never saw before, to see her eat lobster salad.'[4] But still he continued on his social round, enjoying any unexpected glimpses of the hard life of working women which he chanced upon. Here he goes to a house in Inverness Terrace; two of the girls there that night were the 'Miss Griffith-Richardses, with £70,000 each':

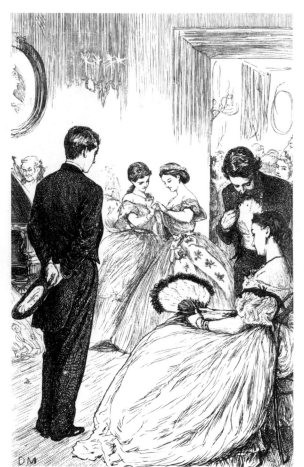

George du Maurier, *'I am spell-bound by the sight of Laura Matilda!'* Illustration from *London Society*, 1865.

My love of suggestive contrasts was gratified at both ends of the evening. Walking up the noble street as I arrived, a kitchenwench was washing dishes in the scullery under the hall steps of a house, within a few doors of where the sumptuous young ladies, my future partners, were disembarking from their carriages at the Pritchards'. I stopped to look at her and them, and speculate on the probable results and values of the two methods of training. Again, as I left to walk home at 2.30, when it was still dark, I saw before me a woman dressed like a coster girl, with a large empty basket on her arm, striding heavily along – From behind, she looked old and worn; but she was young, a stout wench of eighteen. I asked why she was out so late – she answered respectfully – To her it was not late, but early: she had had her night's rest already; had gone to bed at half past six, and got up at two; and was now walking in from Shepherd's Bush, a mile beyond, to Farringdon Market, to buy watercresses – She would then walk back, be home between 6 and 7, have some breakfast (she had had no food as yet) and go out to sell her cresses from house to house. She goes to bed between 6 and 8 – sometimes as late as 8.30 – and rises between two and four. She could not understand that a party – 'parting' she called it – should be so late: could scarce believe that my night's rest was yet to come, any more than I could that hers was already over. Were we not very antipodes of each other? And could any difference be greater, than between this girl and the girls I had just left in the ball room? But her companionship in its way was as interesting as theirs.'[5]

Vast differences in wealth and status separated these women. On one side of the divide was the fashionable lady, who began her day at noon and spent her time riding in her carriage to pay visits and leave cards, dressing for dinner, going to an opera or concert, and then attending a ball until the small hours.

The rigours of such an existence are picked out in du Maurier's *Punch* cartoon 'Rose-Leaf Crumples'. Edith exclaims 'Oh dear! I *am* so tired!' Her 'Loving Husband' asks 'What has fatigued you, my pippetywippety poppet?' and she replies 'Oh! I have had to hold up my parasol all the time I was in the carriage!' On the other side of the divide were working women such as Hannah West, a ballast digger of Upnor, beyond Chatham. Her job was to claw down clay from a quarry face with a pickaxe, load it with a spade into a barrow, and wheel the barrowload of clay down to the riverside wharf where vessels moored to take on ballast. She earned one penny for every ton shifted; one ton meant eight barrowloads of clay. As she told Munby, 'I can only earn a shilling a day, Sir, . . . *twelve tons is as much as I can dig in a day*.'[6] The emphasis is Munby's. It is difficult to take in such extremes, let alone attempt to justify the structure of a society which could allow them to co-exist. Munby lets the bare facts speak for themselves, only commenting that 'A strong homely simple woman, going about the hard work of common life in the midst of idleness and luxury, is to me an object of the highest interest.'[7]

He was always aware that there was a dark side to the glittering and imposing façade of fashionable society. Here he investigates behind the scenes at Rouget's restaurant off Leicester Square:

I clambered down a dark stair into the low rude foulsmelling cellars. Through a gap in some of the rotten old wood partitions, an arm and hand were visible – wet, dirty, muscular, apparently a man's – holding a ragged cloth. Their owner peeped round the corner, hearing me: their owner was a young woman, and comely and robust enough. She was washing the plates from which I and other strangers had just eaten: she was the scullion. I considered her a moment, as one may well do, though she is thought too low for notice. She stood at a sink, behind a wooden dresser packed with choppers and stained with blood and grease, upon which were piles of coppers and saucepans that she had to scour, piles of dirty dishes that she had to wash: her frock and cap, her face and arms, were more or less wet, soiled, perspiring, and her apron was a piece of sacking, wet and filthy, tied round her with a cord. The den where she wrought was low, damp, illsmelling; windowless, lighted by a flaring gas-jet: and, full in view she had on one side a larder hung with raw meat, on the other a common urinal; besides the many ugly dirty implements around her. Here, and thus, dirty in person and clothes, doing the loathsomest work, with none but foul sights and smells about her, this young woman, like thousands of others, stands alone and labours, from noon till near ten at night. Gentlemen, ladies, dine comfortably in comfortable rooms over head, waited on by blackcoated waiters: they walk away, never know that down in that cellar she is doing the foul work which they have made necessary: if they did know it, they would only pass by disgusted, unreflecting.

Munby visits the cellars, but his position is ambiguous. He has no doubt dined well and has then deliberately sought out the woman with the worst job in the establishment. Yet, speaking for her, he asserts that she is not unhappy: 'Does she envy the blackcoated waiters, or contrast her lot with that of the diners upstairs, or get unhappy by reason of the foulness of her work, her person, her wretched den? Bien au contraire! She neither feels, nor is,

ROSE-LEAF CRUMPLES.
Edith. 'Oh Dear! I *am* so tired!'
Loving Husband. 'What has fatigued you, my pippetywippety poppet?'
Edith. 'Oh! I have had to hold up my parasol all the time I was in the carriage!'
Punch cartoon by George du Maurier, 1876.

degraded. As for her dirt, she cannot help it: as for her work, it is her duty, and she is used to it: as for the place, her master put her there, and she is not fastidious.'[8] Munby is no radical social reformer. For him the class system is a complex fixed structure, which allows those above to investigate those below, but which must be maintained for the sake of a properly ordered society. In vain did he address a meeting at the Working Women's College on 'The beauty of manual labour, and the weakness of being ashamed of it'.[9] The working girls there were not susceptible to the romantic ideals of labour Munby conjured up when given the chance, and no doubt had their own ideas on 'the beauty of manual labour' which they were too polite or afraid to voice in public.

Munby was often to be found among what he called 'the sparkling froth atop of society' – a froth which never worried much about the dregs beneath. But his investigations did not allow him the luxury of sublime ignorance. As a single man walking alone through the centre of London late at night after evenings out, Munby was used to being accosted by prostitutes. One such encounter threw up an unexpected revelation:

In Regent Street I was followed by two shabby furtive looking girls, and importuned in the usual manner. But they were not prostitutes – oh no! They were workgirls, working at Michell's the artificial florist in Oxford Street: and when work is slack, they turn out on the streets for a living. Now Michell's is the fashionable shop to which I went, with Ned Anderson and Cuy and Fanny Meredith and other bridesmaids, to buy wreaths and veils for Ned's wedding. A sumptuous drawing-room it was, adorned with flowers and lace and female fripperies; elegant shop nymphs sailing about, serving you with bows and smiles, holding forth sweetly on the proper tints and alternations of the bridesmaids' costume. And *this* is the *other side* of that picture![10]

A little further along his way home he overtook a young widow, aged thirty-one, who was returning from her work as a milliner. She had two children to keep and during the London social 'season' was able to get only about four hours sleep a night. As she said to Munby, 'ladies dont think what women have to go through'.

Tenniel's *Punch* cartoon titled 'The Haunted Lady, or "The Ghost" in the Looking-Glass' points to the plight of the needlewomen. 'Madame La Modiste' is saying: 'We would not have disappointed your ladyship, at any sacrifice, and the robe is finished *à merveille*.' It was published a few weeks after a twenty-year-old seamstress named Mary Ann Walkley had died after working twenty-six and a half hours without break. Overwork and a lack of ventilation were said to have killed her. For a moment the ghost appeared in the mirror and the demands of one section of society were seen to extort the sacrifices of another. The London 'season' consisted of the three or four months between March and July, and during this period a normal working day for a dressmaker was anything from fourteen to twenty hours, and in extreme cases even more. Dress was so linked to status that the demands of

THE HAUNTED LADY,
OR 'THE GHOST' IN THE LOOKING-
GLASS.
Madame La Modiste. 'We would not have
disappointed your Ladyship, at any
sacrifice, and the robe is finished *à
merveille.*'
Punch cartoon by John Tenniel,
published 4 July 1863.

fashion were thought by some to be of paramount importance. A lady would place an order at tea-time – 4 p.m. – for a ball dress to be sent home that same night – 'any time before 12 would do'. And a silk dress took between eight and nine hours to sew by hand.[11] 'Women are the slave drivers' commented one male employer: 'A lady ordered a dress last season, and was told that they must sit up all night to make it. All she said was, "I hope it will fit." The girls were so vexed.'[12]

The seamstresses had a martyr in Mary Ann Walkley, but Society was set in its ways, and the season of course – once the frisson of social conscience had passed – continued as before. The ladies rustled by in their splendid 'creations' as the sun shone and the band played. Here is Munby musing on the passing scene at a Flower Show in the Botanical Gardens:

There is a certain vain and selfconscious pleasure, and also a genuine and unaffected though superficial enjoyment, in 'swelling' about, eating ices or listening to the band, among a brilliant throng, in a lovely garden, on a Summer afternoon: and the sight of pretty girlish faces and tasteful dress is pleasant; and so are the little greetings and confabs with one's acquaintance. But to be often among scenes which are wellknown and always alike; which have nothing to show but a dead level of serene gentility, with no picturesque ruggedness of aspect, no salient trait of character, to catch the mind's eye; that would indeed make one wish for some pricks to kick against. Good heavens! to have married Laura Matilda and all her relations, and found life one vast platitude of tarlatan* and small talk and pap![13]

*Tarlatan is a type of thin, open muslin which was used in the making of ball-dresses.

Pen and ink sketch by Munby. He did not give it a title, and it is undated.

FACT AND FICTION;
or, Ye Bonny Fishwives of Scarborough and their imitators.
Punch cartoon by George du Maurier, 1871.

Society valued young ladies who dressed well, behaved correctly and maintained the 'dead level of serene gentility'. Munby found his heroines among working women who dressed according to the demands of their job and not the demands of fashion. The Wigan pit brow lasses and the Scarborough fishergirls presented alternatives to the values and lifestyle offered by London society. The contrast of class, of sturdiness and of dress is seen in Munby's drawing of a young lady in a crinoline confronting a pit girl in trousers who is about to oil the wheels of an upended wagon. Similarly, in du Maurier's drawing for *Punch*, titled 'Fact and Fiction; or, ye bonny fishwives of Scarborough and their imitators', class faces class; 'real' women face their puny counterfeits in fashionable dress.

Munby arranged two small, folding photograph mounts to display class differences and to embody 'suggestive contrasts'. These he probably took with him when travelling in this country and abroad. In the first mount we see on the left a working girl, a domestic servant, dressed in a bonnet and shawl, and carrying a wicker basket. Facing her on the right is a young woman in an elegant dress. In the second mount, on the left, is a lady in a hat photographed 'à la Gainsborough'; on the right is a woman posing as a grimy chimney sweep, naked to the waist and wearing a chain round her neck, and a strap around her wrist. All four photographs are of the same woman – a woman who for Munby combined in herself the refined nature of a true-born lady and the honest, hardworking straightforwardness which he so admired in working women. This was the woman whom he chose in place of 'Laura Matilda'. Her name was Hannah Cullwick; she was that most lowly creature among the ranks of domestic servants – a maid-of-all-work. And Munby married her in 1873.

'Suggestive contrasts' seen in the person of Hannah, on the left as a working girl and on the right as a fashionable young lady.
Two photographs in one of Munby's travelling mounts.

'Suggestive contrasts' of a more extreme nature in another of Munby's travelling mounts. On the left a portrait of Hannah photographed 'à la Gainsborough', and on the right Hannah posing black and naked to the waist as a chimney sweep.

Hannah Cullwick was a Shropshire girl who began her life in service as housemaid to Lady Boughey of Aqualate Hall, Newport, and later became a scullion with Lady Louisa Cotes, the daughter of Lord Liverpool. Her duties brought her to London for the season, and it was in London in 1854 that she first met Munby. By the following year their friendship was such that she accepted an invitation to visit him in the Temple. She took a job in Suffolk, and Munby travelled down to see her. Things became easier when, in 1856, she returned to London to work as a general servant, and Munby was able to meet her several times a week. Her master was for three years a Mr. Jackson, who was in the upholstery business. When he became 'poorer through extravagance' and had to leave his business and move outside London, she got a place at a house opposite belonging to Mr. Foster, a beermerchant, so that she could stay close to Munby. For the next ten years she had to overcome many difficulties to continue meeting Munby, whom she called Massa – master. Their 'courtship', if such it can be called, lasted nineteen years, and had to be conducted furtively. Moments together were stolen moments and all the more highly charged emotionally because of the secrecy. Here Munby pays Hannah a visit in the late 1850s:

She was then a general servant in a tradesman's well to do family at Kilburn; and one day, I went to see her, at her own suggestion, in her master's house, for the family were all absent, and she wished to show me her work, and the places where she worked. She showed me the kitchen she had to scour; the big kitchen grate that she blacked, the chimney that she swept, the scullery where she cleaned the sink, the hole in which she cleaned the boots and knives; and the scenes of many another sordid but necessary task. And she took me upstairs and showed me her attic, a little bare room, with a blue-check quilt on the bed, and one chair, and a common washing stand in the corner, with jug and basin; 'what I never use,' said she, 'for you know I always wash me at the sink.' There was no looking glass in the room: she seldom used one. Then, as we came downstairs, she opened, by way of contrast, the door of her mistress's luxurious bedroom. On the bed lay a ball dress, of black gauze and lace, with crimson garniture; and this made me wish to see for once how Hannah would look in a lady's condition. I told her to put on the ball dress. She hesitated to profane the Missis's things by touching them, much more, by wearing them; but to please me, she consented. She took off her own servant's dress, and put on that of her mistress. It was too short and too narrow for her, and it would not meet around her healthy rustic waist; still, she was able to wear it; and, seeing a rose in the room, I brushed out her bright hair in a lady's fashion, and placed the rose within it. Thus she stood before me to be looked at; smiling and slightly blushing; feeling awkward and strange, in that unknown garb, but looking not awkward at all, but most graceful. I gazed on her in a kind of rapture: so lovely a figure she was, so ladylike, so sweet, that I longed 'to take her away from her slavery', and make of her a lady indeed. 'And now, dear,' at last I said, 'turn round, and look at yourself.' She wondered what I meant; for she had forgotten, that behind her stood a large cheval glass, capable of showing her from top to toe. But she turned round, and saw herself reflected at full length in the mirror. The effect of this revelation was startling. It was not her beauty, that struck; nor yet the sight of herself in a garb she had never worn before: but now for the first time she noticed that her neck and bosom, and even her shoulders, were bare. Dazzling white, they seemed, by contrast with her hardworking arms, which of course were also bare: but in an instant, they were suffused, like her face, with one universal blush – celestial rosyred, Love's proper hue. She shut her eyes, turned sharply from the glass, and suddenly flung herself into my arms – 'that I might rather feel than see the beating of her heart.' 'Oh Massa', she whispered, 'I am naked!'

Never before had I felt so strongly the need of self control in her presence: never, before or since, have I been filled with a more passionate ardour of love and reverence for that pure and innocent soul, who had trusted herself so utterly to me. I soothed and comforted and at length released her; but nothing could induce her to look at the glass again. She tore off that strange and shameful finery; she put on again her own cotton frock and servant's cap and apron; she hurried me down to her kitchen, where only she could feel properly clad, and at home.

And it was this incident, more than any other thing, that made me wholly and for ever hers.[14]

The incident points to the attractions Munby found in his relationship with Hannah. She was a strong, tall, handsome woman, capable of hard physical work, but with a very kind, loving, gentle nature; a working-class woman who could undertake the most filthy jobs and yet remain 'uncoarsened', displaying the sensitivity and refinement of character which at that time was usually associated only with ladies.

The change of dress which so roused Munby also symbolised a change of class, and it was the class differences between them which delayed their marriage for so long. When at last they married in 1873, both knew that theirs was – according to the rules of society – a *mésalliance*, which was bound to bring uncomfortable social pressures to bear on both partners. Such marriages were comparatively uncommon, and the crossing of class boundaries was always a subject of interest and gossip for those who set great store by the rigid divisions of society and by the social niceties and formalised behaviour which shored up the system.

In 1863 Munby was drawn into conversation with a Miss Williams on Lord Robert Montagu's recent marriage with a housemaid: 'She refused to believe that any such woman could by [any] possibility be refined in nature, or be companionable for a man of education. She knew them by experience: their faces might be pretty and their manner modest, but within, they were full of baseness and vulgarity. And no man of refinement and gentlemanly feeling could *ever* degrade himself by such an union. . . . No words could express Miss Williams's disgust at that proceeding. "You, for instance" said she "I am sure *you* never would stoop to look twice at such a being!"'[15] Hannah discussed the same subject with a Mrs. Davis, who had been a nursemaid; she recorded in her diary that: 'at teatime she began about Marrying, and how Lord R. Montagu had married his nursemaid and that – what a fine thing it was to Marry Well as she call'd it, and when i said love and honour and one's word was more than riches she laugh'd at me – Cause she said what odds if the girl had had another sweetheart anywhere – she had seen more of the world than i had and she would always give one thing up for a better.' Hannah, not out to ensnare Munby, commented: 'Mrs. Davis, poor woman, seems as worldly minded as possible and rather vulgar i think.'[16]

Munby, who was forty-four when he married Hannah, realised the implications of the step he was taking. Eliza Lynn Linton, who was later to become friendly with Munby but knew nothing of Hannah, had some sensible general observations to make in an article published in 1868: 'Love-marriages, made against the will of the parents before the character is formed, and while the obligations of society are still unrealized, are generally *mésalliances* founded on passion and fancy only. A man or woman of mature age who knows what he or she wants may make a *mésalliance*, but it is made with a full understanding and deliberate choice; and, if the thing turns out badly, they can blame themselves less for precipitancy than for wrong calculation. The man of fifty who marries his cook knows what he most values in women. It is not manners, and it is not accomplishments; perhaps it is usefulness, perhaps good-temper; at all events it is something that the cook has and that the ladies of his acquaintance have not, and he is content to take the disadvantages of his choice with its advantages.'[17] One disadvantage was that Munby could never bring himself to acknowledge his wife – who masqueraded as his servant – openly in public. To all outside appearances his batchelor's existence continued as before. To make such a disclosure could obviously play havoc with the polite conventions of society. Munby told the story of Lord Westmeath who married (and later divorced) a housemaid, wooing her with such blandishments as 'Wont you have a coronet, Betty?' to which she replied in all innocence, 'What's that Sir?': 'After her marriage, her old mistress, who did not know of her rise, met her coming out of Howell & James's;* and not observing – strange to say – how she was drest, said "Well, Betty, I'm glad to see you – come and see me at my hotel". The next day, a card was sent up – "The Marchioness of Westmeath"; and in walked Betty. "You see I'm come to call on you Ma'am" said the Marchioness.'[18]

Munby used to watch Hannah at a distance as she cleaned the steps and flags of the house where she was a servant, and commented: 'What a shame it seemed that she should have such things to do – that she, with her tall graceful figure and with a face for all the world like Lady Constance Grosvenor's, the reigning beauty of that time, should not only be a servant, but the lowest servant, a kitchendrudge! How I chafed in secret that I could not take her away and give her the rank that seemed her due!'[19] And again: 'Most sad, to see her wearing out her youth in such sordid drudgery, her only haunts the kitchen the scullery and the coalcellar! She unconsciously increased this sadness in me, by bringing out a portrait of herself, taken five years ago, and looking all tenderness and refinement. Then, if I had had the means, she might have passed into a drawingroom at once: now, it is too

*Howell, James & Co. ran a fashionable shop selling silks and jewellery in Regent Street.

late.'[20] This was written in 1860, and for years Munby remained in confusion and self-doubt as to the final outcome of his relationship with Hannah.

John Duguid Milne, who made a study of the position of women in mid-Victorian society, described the problems of middle-class men of the period in forming relationships with women: 'The stiffness and reserve between the sexes, in the middle ranks, brought about by the separation of their education, of their daily interests and pursuits, cause young men to undervalue women of their own rank; and, finding little pleasure in their society, little room for the natural flow of impressions and feelings, they seek such vent elsewhere; in the more unrestrained and artless intercourse of a lower rank, or in the ruder companionships of their own sex. If young men and young women of the middle ranks had more the means of forming friendships one with another, it would be better for society in many ways. If a man esteem female character in his own rank, is it not likely that he will respect it in an inferior rank? At present a man fails to find a true companion among women of his own status; and, believing them less capable of such companionship than with all their disadvantages they really are, he treats one class with injustice, and is tempted to wrong another still more deeply.'[21] These perceptive remarks throw light on both Munby's relationship with Hannah and on the enthusiasm and sense of relief he felt when talking to girls in Wigan or Filey. Young ladies were skilled at 'saying nothings prettily':

'And then, of course, I have to read,
To get up a sensation,
Something at least that may begin
The business of flirtation;
A run-away, or convent "case,"
A novel, or a play
Against the evening; some there are
(Bores rather!) who will say,
After the usual "Are you fond
Of music?" "Do you care
For flowers?" "Have you read this or that?"
And so I must prepare
For small talk, of all kinds: true art
Will make one's knowledge go
Quite far enough; enough to make
A fashionable show.'[22]

In the face of such mindlessly genteel femininity, it is hardly surprising that men looked for 'real' women elsewhere and, as Milne warned, were tempted 'to wrong' working-class women.

Munby talked to factory girls who worked for Messrs. Platt and Barlow of Bolton, who were in London demonstrating cotton spinning and muslin weaving machinery at the International Exhibition of 1862. One of them:

surprised me with a disgusting fact: to wit, that whilst at her work here in the exhibition, she has many times been solicited by well-drest men to go home with them or meet them after dark for an evil purpose. 'Why, it's nobbut two ahrs ago, Ah wer spoke to like that; a gentleman comes up, and white hair he had too, he were sixty if he wer a day, and a fine man as you'd like to see; and he begins asking ma' aboot machine, and while Ah wor a'telling him he took on wi summat quite different: an' thinks I, Ah'll just see what a does mean afore Ah says aht. Sae Ah answered him civil like, and at last he says "Will ye meet mah toneet, ma' dear" – sau then Ah ups and says Get oot, ye auld rascal! and Ah ton'd o' my heel and left him'.

She added that she did not believe there was one of the factory girls in the building who had not been insulted in the same way.[23]

As a girl who sold oranges in Albany Street, London once told the painter W. P. Frith, trouble usually came not from ordinary passers-by or idlers, but from 'swells'. 'Gentlemen', she concluded, 'is much greater blackguards than what blackguards is.'[24]

It is difficult to follow what happened in the years before Munby's marriage as he cut many references to Hannah out of his diaries. In 1894 he noted that these excised passages 'described the hours we spent together; the training and teaching that I gave her; and the work, often of the lowest and most servile kind, which she – a maid-of-all-work – of her own accord did for me, to show her love in her own way.'[25] Having decided that 'we must create our Utopia out of the materials at hand' he seems to have set out to make a lady of Hannah by 'the ordinary methods of education'. This proving impractical, he began to evolve his 'great experiment': 'she was to become, and she *has* become, a noble and gentle woman, not only without the aid of technical helps, but in spite of ignorance and lowly isolation, and *by means* of that very toil and servile labour which is supposed to make a woman contemptible and vulgar. Physical degradation was to be the channel, and even the source of spiritual beauty. It has often been so, among religious women of old: but, with an English maid servant, how would it be?'[26] On one occasion Hannah had undressed and 'got on a stool and up the chimney out o sight': 'The soot was thick all round, and soft and warm and i lay in it and fetch'd a shower or two down wi my arms, and it trickl'd over like a bath – i stopped in the chimney and thought about Massa and how he'd enjoy seein me when i got down and all that, and wonder'd what he was doing and then i come down – it seem'd quite cold out o the chimney and i got into the water [in a bath] and wash'd me – it took me a good while to get clean and the water i made thick and black. i just put on my shift and petticoat and bundled my other clothes up and run to bed – Massa wrote after and said at the very time i was in the chimney he was at a ball, and among ladies with white necks and arms and all so grand, and how he look'd at them and thought of me the while, and he could well imagine the contrast as he'd seen me so often.'[27] Three years previously Munby had had himself photographed with her in the guise of a chimney-sweep – 'her noblest guise': 'she was taken in [that] black and forlorn condition, crouching on the ground at my feet – I doing my best to look down upon her like a tyrant! That was for "the contrast": Contrast indeed – but which the nobler?'[28]* This is the twilight area of Munby's relationship with Hannah: strange rituals seem to hint at strange pleasures. As Munby removed so much of the evidence from the diary, we get only glimpses of his liaison with Hannah, who emerges as a woman of seemingly infinite patience

*It is probable that this photograph is the one reproduced above. The original is cut down, and the toe of a man's shoe can be seen on the right.

and love. She let him cut her hair short like a man's, and wore a neck-chain and wrist-strap as signs of slavery. She washed his feet, picked him up and carried him around the room in an amorous hug, sat him on her knee for a little 'petting', and together they went through the yearly ritual of 'adding up the boots' – Munby calculated that during 1861 Hannah had cleaned 1,023 pairs of boots.[29] Occasionally he must have realised how hard Hannah was working. On a visit to a female prison he complained to the Matron that the convicts were having an easy time of it. Hannah had to work much harder.

But life was not all drudgery. In August 1873 he travelled with her on a ten-day tour of France. For this Hannah assumed the rôle of a lady – they had been married seven months – and Munby provided her with suitable clothing: 'He bought me a felt hat and plume of cock's feathers to wear, and a veil, and a new brooch to pin my shawl with, and a new waterproof cloak, but i generally wore my blue skirt and jacket over my grey frock, with frill round my neck, and white cuffs, and grey kid gloves, and carrying my striped sunshade – all so different to anything i had got used to . . .'[30] The trip was a great success, but the return to London demanded of Hannah another rôle change: 'At 6 a.m. the train for London started; and Hannah, seating herself, said with a smile "Well, Massa, my lady-days are over now!" At Charing Cross . . . she took off her charming felt hat and veil, put on her old servant's strawbonnet, which had lain in my knapsack all through our tour, concealed her other splendours under a large plaid shawl, took off her gloves, and carrying a bag in her bare hands, went quietly home, like a servant, to the empty house.'[31] Munby expected her to be able to switch from servant to lady and back again with little effort, and one can only marvel that she was able to cope with such drastic changes as confidently as she did. The following year Munby wanted to take her 'as a lady' to the Welsh border, or alternatively for them to tramp together as a working man and woman. Hannah laughed at Munby's thinking he could pass himself off as a working man, and said she didn't want to go – 'I've been out enough.'[32]

Before their marriage she would visit him, usually on Sundays, and he would select and read to her poetry and extracts from novels. On these occasions Hannah would 'make herself useful' by washing his feet, making cigars for him, mending his coat or sewing a new buttonhole for his shirt, cutting the pages of books and generally taking every opportunity to ensure that her beloved Massa was happy and comfortable: 'Her notion of love is *doing* things: a useful practical notion! "You see" she triumphantly exclaimed, after some new service – "I can do *everything* for you!" Surely a most pure unselfish triumph! To look upon oneself as made for another, to have no pleasure but in doing his bidding and serving him – none but a woman, one fancies, is capable of such devotion. Applied to its highest Object, this is the very principle of Christian self sacrifice.'[33] At such moments Hannah embodied the ideal of the wife-servant, and seems to be playing the

Girl selling shrimps in a London street. By R. L. Sims, 1884.

PEFFERLAW PUBLIC LIBRARY

rôle laid down for women by Jean-Jacques Rousseau a century earlier in *Émile*: 'A woman's education must . . . be planned in relation to man. To be pleasing in his sight, to win his respect and love, to train him in childhood, to tend him in manhood, to counsel and console, to make his life pleasant and happy, these are the duties of woman for all time, and this is what she should be taught while she is young. . . . [Girls] must be trained to bear the yoke from the first, so that they may not feel it, to master their own caprices and to submit themselves to the will of others.'[34]

Mary Wollstonecraft's response to this, thirty years later in her *Vindication of the Rights of Woman* (1792), was 'What nonsense!' But there were some who took his advice very seriously. In her *Essays on Woman's Work* (1865) Bessie Rayner Parkes told of Thomas Day, a gentleman who dreamed that he could create an ideal woman, bent only upon serving him, through the educational theories of Rousseau. However odd Munby's theories of 'educating' Hannah were, they were not unique. Thomas Day was born in 1748. Having been thwarted in love, and despairing of finding another woman to fulfil his dreams, he decided to educate one for that very purpose. He was twenty-one when he selected two twelve-year-old girls, both of them beautiful – a blonde from an orphan asylum at Shrewsbury, whom he called Sabrina, and an auburn brunette from the Foundling Hospital in London, who was given the name Lucretia. His choice of a wife was to be made within a year, and, Sabrina eventually being chosen, Lucretia was apprenticed to a milliner:

He then devoted himself to make Sabrina a perfect woman; but none of his experiments had the success he wished. 'Her spirit could not be armed against the dread of pain and the appearance of danger, a species of courage which with him was a *sine qua non* in the character of a wife. When he dropped melted sealing-wax upon her arms she did not endure it heroically; nor when he fired pistols at her petticoats, which she believed to be charged with balls, could she refrain from starting aside, or suppress her screams.' He invented secrets, and found she betrayed them to the servants and her playfellows; he gave her no rewards, and excluded her from the knowledge of the value of money, or the admiration bestowed upon beauty; he cut off remorselessly all the little outward incentives to good behaviour, leaving her none but that of pleasing him, though the poor child appears not to have had a notion of his good intentions; and, of course, 'fear had greatly the ascendant of affection,' or, as we should say, poor little Sabrina became horribly afraid of him.

Mr. Day despaired of his pupil-wife, abandoned his plans, and sent her off to boarding school. When he eventually did marry another woman, he made 'frequent experiments on her temper and her attachment'. The end of Thomas Day was not without grim irony: 'It was extremely characteristic of Mr. Day that he should have been killed by a kick administered by a favourite foal, which he had reared, fed, and trained, but which objected to the bit when its master, "disdaining to employ a horse-breaker," undertook the task himself.'[35]

Munby, too, came to realise his mistake in thinking that he could shape another human being into a form which would please him. It would have been easier if he had been able to decide whether he wanted Hannah to be a perfect lady or a refined chimneysweep. As he seems to have wanted both, his 'great experiment' was doomed to failure, as was his marriage – that final drastic attempt to resolve the problems he saw before them. As Munby did not disclose his marriage, they were never able to set up house together and it is unlikely that he ever really wanted to. He wrote little of his deteriorating relationship with Hannah, but the indications are that the strains were too great; they seem to have quarrelled, and although they remained close in spirit, they spent much of the next thirty years apart.*

As he grew towards old age, Munby looked back on an ideal vision of how things should have been, and no doubt mistook the vision for reality:

For this marriage of theirs was not a marriage of convenience, nor even a love-match between equals. It was a marriage of two who came together as it were from opposite poles, with a full and lasting conviction that they were made for each other; and that the contrast between them in station, in knowledge and experience, in outward seeming, was itself an evidence of the fact. It was a marriage of two enthusiasts: she, an enthusiast for her own class and calling, its ways, its dress, its manners; he, a sharer in that enthusiasm of hers, and an idealist, to whom she was the only woman who could fulfil his ideal and who did fulfil it. [36]

*They had married in 1873. Hannah died aged seventy-six in 1909, and Munby died in the following year.

3: Who Should Wear the Trousers?

'The principle which regulates the existing social relations between the two sexes – the legal subordination of one sex to the other – is wrong in itself and now one of the chief hindrances to human improvement, and . . . ought to be replaced by a principle of perfect equality, admitting no power or privilege on the one side nor disability on the other.'   John Stuart Mill, *The Subjection of Women*, (1869).

Listen females all,
 No matter what your trade is,
Old Nick is in the girls
 The d——l's in the ladies;

Married men may weep
 And tumble in the ditches
Since women are resolved,
 To wear the shirt and breeches.

from *I'll be a Bloomer*,
a popular song dating from the 1850s.

WHEN Munby was making his way home through central London late at night after a ball or a party, he encountered the 'strolling prostitutes' who were always there in large numbers looking for clients. They wore gaudy bonnets, velvet mantles, thin boots and pink silk stockings: 'As to those pink stockings, I could not but think as I saw them how great is the power of purity and the influence of motive, in such matters. This harlot lifts her dress to the calf to excite your passions; and they *are* excited.' Munby contrasts this reaction to that when he visits Boulogne to observe and talk with the *pêcheuses* – the shrimpgirls – who 'walk in broad daylight along the crowded quay, barefoot, and barelegged to the very thigh, and yet no one shall even think of indecency.'[1] Munby sought to dissociate his heroic working girls from the tainted world of sexual desire, but in fact it seems likely that he was strongly attracted to them by their physical attributes, as well as by their engaging and unsophisticated characters, and by his interest in the details of their jobs. Their attractiveness was probably all the greater because they did not knowingly make themselves alluring for him, and simply dressed and acted as they normally did. It was a case of 'evil be to him who evil thinks', and du Maurier's *Punch* cartoon which bears the significant title '*Honi Soit*,' &c., depicts an alternative, prudish view of the way that the Boulogne *pêcheuses* dressed. The caption tells us that Ann and Sarah see some fishwomen 'clothed *that* indelicate that you might have knocked them down with a feather!'

'HONI SOIT,' &c.
*Ann and Sarah see some Fishwomen
'Clothed that indelicate that you might have
knocked them down with a feather!'*
Punch *cartoon by George du Maurier,*
1866. The scene is the quayside at
Boulogne.

Another contemporary reference indicates that their reaction was the more common. The fame was widespread of these fishwomen 'at whose legs [young Englishmen] take much . . . pleasure to regard all the day at Dieppe and Boulogne.'[2]

Munby observed them at work and always attempted to smother desire with objective observations and hearty descriptions of their very hard work when they were in deep water: 'How picturesque they looked, stooping under their baskets, and trotting in regular beat along the sunny sands! And when they came to a landlocked pool, the pack would plunge in, delighting in the cool water, and lifting their scanty kilts to the hips showing a white thigh strangely different from the sunburnt leg below. But with instinctive modesty they dropped their ragged skirts again as they came near.'[3] On one occasion he went for a walk along the deserted pier, and watched the moon rise from dark clouds over the town. A fishwoman came up to him and 'proposed a walk and "pleasure" on the beach'. He was astonished, blamed her corruption on 'us English', and went up to his room to cool himself on this sultry July night by sitting naked at his window 'on Shelley's "airbath" principle'.*[4]

*Shelley maintained 'that the depravity of the physical and moral nature of man originated in his unnatural habits of life'. Accordingly, he warned against eating meat, drinking 'spirituous liquors', and 'muffling . . . our bodies in superfluous apparel'. (*Notes* to *Queen Mab*, 1813).

Munby's observation of working women outside London was concerned in part at least with their physical appearance. The Wigan pit brow girls wore trousers and at a distance looked like men; the Yorkshire fishergirls gathered up their dresses and petticoats and tied them around each knee to make improvised trousers whilst working on the slippery shore; and the Boulogne *pêcheuses* wore short skirts. He made at least one journey specially to see working women wearing trousers; in 1861 he travelled almost two hundred miles to Lympstone in Devon where women in canvas trousers gathered mussels, cockles and oysters.

In the 1850s Mrs. Dexter C. Bloomer of New York had attempted to introduce her Bloomer costume with its loose pantaloons reaching to the ankle. Englishwomen seem to have been both shocked and amused by the outfit. The most interesting reaction was that which associated woman's wearing of trousers with her appropriating the dominant rôle of the man. 'Bloomerism' gave John Leech an opportunity to explore in his *Punch* cartoons the idea of women 'wearing the trousers', and, as if inspired by doing so, rising to usurp the rule of men. These Leech cartoons show the imagined repercussions of such a move towards liberating women in society. In one a 'superior creature' – a woman – proposes marriage to a gentleman who bashfully toys with his food, and murmurs 'You must really ask Mamma!', who appears, suitably outraged and similarly arrayed in Bloomer costume, in the doorway. In the second, the girls enjoy a smoke together and act as 'fast gents' – independent and out to enjoy themselves. Mrs. Bloomer was an active supporter of the emancipation of women, and the public attention aroused by her championing of 'male attire' for females was an indication of the growing interest in the reassessment of the rôle of women in society. The strength of the reaction to 'Bloomerism' may also have indicated an awareness of the gravity of the possible threat to man's domination of mid-Victorian society. It is ironic that the remote possibility of the Bloomer costume becoming anything more than a nine days' wonder was scotched after it had been seen to be worn by working women. In 1851 a London brewery dressed all the company's barmaids in the costume, and effectively killed it off as a possible 'fashion'.[5] Looking back in 1872, a writer in *The Saturday Review* commented that Bloomerism 'wilfully violated the whole ethics of costume; it set women in a kind of travestied antagonism to men, the ladies' coats and pants being only the outward and visible signs of the inward unnatural rivalry that animated the fair reformers; it made the exercise of woman's natural religion, beauty, impossible; and it ended in collapse, as it was sure to do.'[6] Nevertheless, the link between trousers and the emancipation of women was to be kept alive by all the later movements which sought to clothe women in more 'rational' or 'hygienic' dress.

Polite society could not accept women in trousers, and an article on 'Costume and its Morals' in 1867 referred to 'those limbs which it is still

forbidden to expose absolutely'. Not only were trousers unacceptable, the word 'trousers' was itself usually circumvented by the use of some mealy-mouthed synonym, of which there were several – 'unmentionables', 'continuations' or even 'non-talk-aboutables'. It is difficult to gauge how much one was supposed to smile when one mouthed these absurdities – in fact it seems likely that they were usually to be found in printed rather than spoken form.[7] Society ladies conspired with fashion to pretend that they had no legs, and propelled themselves smoothly under cover of their crinolines as if on castors.

And yet it was perfectly acceptable to expose the breasts. Of a dance at a friend's house in 1863 Munby wrote: 'I danced but once – with a very pretty and intelligent girl; married, I think: whose fair bare bosom, as she stood beside me, was open to all men's gaze; and could not but attract that of her partner, for its tracery of soft blue veins blushed – so to speak – through the transparent snowy skin, like delicate marble. This, and the crowd of naked female shoulders that hemmed me in on all sides, reminds one how thoroughly conventional, in such matters, is modesty.'[8] The writer of the article on 'Costume and its Morals' observed that 'it is in evening costume that our women have reached the minimum of dress and the maximum of brass. We remember a venerable old lady whose ideas of decorum were such that in her speech all above the foot was ankle, and all below the chin was chest; but now the female bosom is less the subject of a revelation than the feature of an exposition, and charms that were once reserved are now made the common property of every looker on. A costume which has been described as consisting of a smock, a waistband, and a frill seems to exceed the bounds of honest liberality, and resembles most perhaps the attire mentioned

ONE OF THE DELIGHTFUL RESULTS OF BLOOMERISM. – THE LADIES WILL POP THE QUESTION
Superior Creature. 'Say! Oh, say, dearest! Will you be mine?' &c., &c.
Punch cartoon by John Leech, 1851.

SOMETHING MORE APROPOS OF BLOOMERISM
(*Behind the Counter is one of the 'Inferior Animals.'*)
Punch cartoon by John Leech, 1851.

by Rabelais, "nothing before and nothing behind, with sleeves of the same." Not very long ago two gentlemen were standing together at the Opera. "Did you ever see anything like that?" inquired one, with a significant glance, directing the eyes of his companion to the uncovered bust of a lady immediately below. "Not since I was weaned," was the suggestive reply.'[9] And yet London ladies who dressed in this way would have condemned a woman in trousers as brazen and immoral.

The 1860s are the years most fully covered by Munby's diaries, and it was during this decade that the debate on woman's place in society was brought to the fore. Munby, able to observe women of all classes, was ideally placed to see the early moves in the long battle to secure women's rights.

The femininity encouraged in the full-bosomed girls of the middle classes who danced with Munby at parties – 'a bevy of women floating in gauze or oscillating in velvet'[10] – was a passive, yielding, submissive femininity. Taught to regard themselves as too 'delicate' to work, these girls could concentrate on the ladylike pursuit of doing nothing, waited on hand and foot by servants. Was this woman's true role in life – watching from the sidelines, and whiling away the hours as best she could? Surely – to take an example from fiction – David Copperfield's wife Dora could have found something more constructive to do than to hold his pens as he wrote? As J. D. Milne commented at the time: 'It is but an equivocal compliment to woman that man should treat her like a doll he is in constant fear of breaking.'[11]

Marriage was still seen as the firm foundation upon which society stood, and the view that 'woman's sphere is the home' was widely held. If women could not go out to work and support themselves by their earnings, marriage and dependence on a husband for support was their only hope. Not surprisingly, feminists such as Josephine Butler spoke out bitterly against the unenviable position in which many women found themselves – trying to ensnare a husband: 'What dignity can there be in the attitude of women in general, and toward men in particular, when marriage is held (and often necessarily so, being the sole means of maintenance) to be the one end of a woman's life, when it is degraded to the level of a feminine profession, when those who are soliciting a place in this profession resemble those flaccid Brazilian creepers which cannot exist without support, and which sprawl out their limp tendrils in every direction to find something – no matter what – to hang upon; when the insipidity or the material necessities of so many women's lives make them ready to accept almost any man who may offer himself?'[12] The question of women and work was made all the more urgent by the fact that women outnumbered men in the mid nineteenth century, and as these hundreds of thousands of 'redundant women' (as they came to be called) could not hope to find husbands, they had to become self-supporting, and find work.[13]

In 1857 Barbara Leigh Smith argued, in *Women and Work*, that it was through work that women could secure their rightful place in society, and that for a woman to work was not to deny her essential femininity:

WORK – not drudgery, but WORK – is the great beautifier. Activity of brain, heart, and limb, gives health and beauty, and makes women fit to be the mothers of children. A listless, idle, empty-brained, empty-hearted, ugly woman has no right to bear children.

To think a woman is more feminine be- cause she is frivolous, ignorant, weak, and sickly, is absurd; the larger-natured a woman is, the more decidedly feminine she will be; the stronger she is, the more strongly femin- ine. You do not call a lioness unfeminine, though she is different in size and strength from the domestic cat, or mouse.[14]

The main question confronting the supporters of work for women was what work would be suitable for them.

The more intelligent and well-educated women were trying to gain entry to the professions. In 1856 Jessie Meriton White was told by St. Bartholomew's Hospital that a female could not be admitted to an examination for a diploma in surgery and midwifery, and she wrote to Barbara Leigh Smith that 'a little alteration in Dr. Johnson's lines gives the only reason why I was denied admission:–

"We shan't admit you, Mistress Fell –
The reason why we cannot tell;
But this we all know very well,
We shan't admit you, Mistress Fell!"'[15]

The battle to secure jobs for the mass of ordinary women was also fought against male opposition, the men trying to keep women out of their trades, often fearing that women would provide a source of cheap labour to compete with their own. Munby came across an instance of this opposition when he visited Copelands Pottery Works at Stoke in 1859: 'An intelligent clerk showed us over: all very interesting . . . A good many women and girls employed; healthy and clean enough, but all plain, and most of them small. They turn the wheel, serve the moulder with clay, print the patterns on dishes, polish the gilding, and do the inferior painting: but they *haven't skill* of hand or mind *for the higher artistic work*. Some few have, but we daren't employ them, the *men wouldn't stand it*. Note this.'[16] An even meaner action of the men in this trade was to forbid women the arm rests they themselves used to ease and simplify their work.[17]

Munby was particularly interested in the women who got round the employment barrier by posing as men. He visited the London courts whenever cases were heard involving women who had pretended to be men, for example in 1861: 'Went out to the Westminster Police Court, to the examination of Mary Newell, the maid of all work who robbed her master last week, went off in man's clothes, travelled down to Yarmouth, took lodgings there, smoked cigars, and made love to her landlady. Assuming that she had as I was told done it only for a lark, I admired her pluck skill and humour, and

FINK.PHOTO.   57.OXFORD ST.

Hannah wearing men's clothes, 1860.
Carte-de-visite portrait by Fink of Oxford
Street.

wished to observe her person and character. But the inspector who helped to catch her showed me that she was probably a practised thief and a dissolute girl.'[18]

In 1866 an especially interesting case took him to the police station at Sittingbourne, where Superintendent Green – 'a stout big bearded man, kindly and lumpish' whom Munby later rewarded with bottles of Burton ale – told him about 'Richard' Bruce, a young woman of twenty-three who had stopped at the local workhouse as a casual tramp, whilst making her way on foot to Dover. There it was discovered that she was a woman dressed as a man, and the police superintendent's wife had given her women's clothes to wear. Munby travelled with the superintendent to Strood, where they found the girl – whose real name was Helen – and heard her story:

Had a fair education: father a shipwright: parents died; became pupilteacher in school at Lynn, her subjects English, geography, music (Yes, I play the piano, Sir): earned little thus, being so young: resolved to be a lad, and earn more: bought men's clothes one by one, put them on secretly out of doors one night and threw her own away: got a steerage passage Lynn to Newcastle (six years ago, and she 17): got work at N[ewcastle] as errand boy to Snowden, grocer, Quayside, and then as shoplad, 18 months: then short time odd boy at the docks: worked her passage as stoker, N[ewcastle] to Leith: got work as tallyman above ground at an ironstone mine somewhere in Lowlands: took ship Leith to Hamburg, in her best coat and trousers, thinking to teach English there: found no employ: came back straight to London, and been living there 3 years up to last Xmas, always in men's clothes, lodging . . .; getting work as she could at copying music, and parts for actors, and writing at times, and doing accounts. At last, thought she would go quite away, to France (speaking French a little) and try her luck as English teacher – *male*, mind: and was walking to Dover accordingly, when caught. This was her story, as she told it me . . . What was she going to do now? Well, has 1/ a day for reading an hour to an old lady, and is writing *religious articles for the Wesleyan New Connexion Magazine*! Will hold on thus a few weeks, then if no more work, means to go into men's clothes again and come up to London for work. Thinks she might get to play piano at Weston's Music Hall, *as a man*. Why not as a woman? 'Oh, the *pay*, Sir! Besides, a woman wants references and all that, and as for accounts, she can't get 'em to do; but when I go as a lad, they just tell me to sit down and do 'em.' What she would like best would be, a clerkship. She 'feels strange' in women's clothes, though getting a little used to them: much prefers men's clothes, and would gladly adopt them for life, having now worn them six years on end.[19]

Superintendent Green advised her to stick to women's clothing, but Munby characteristically told her to please herself about dress.

He was tireless in his pursuit of such cases. In 1871 he wrote to the Chief Superintendent of the Dublin Police for details of 'Patrick McCormack', a labouring 'man' who lived for a time as a married 'man' and who was found to be a woman only after 'his' death in a Dublin workhouse.

Munby did not miss the opportunity to support the right of women to take whatever work they felt to be within their powers: 'I may add that there are scores of women in recent years who have taken to men's work and men's clothing, as bricklayers, grooms, navvies, and what not, in order to obtain that fair wage and that freedom of labour to which they know themselves entitled, though the "women's rights" folk do not seem to know as much.'[20] Probably no one but Munby had collected so much information on this unusual aspect of the struggle to obtain work for women, and only he was prepared to give these cases serious attention – the newspapers seeing nothing but curiosity value in such stories.[21]

Other attemps to find work for women were more orthodox. One line of attack was to seek out jobs held by men which were held to be more suitable for women. Figures were produced from the 1861 census to show how extensively men were employed in occupations which were considered 'essentially womanly'; over forty thousand served behind the counter as drapers, over ten thousand as hairdressers; others made artificial flowers and corsets.

In 1859 Jessie Boucherett had established the Society for Promoting the Employment of Women, and attempted to introduce women into the exclusively male occupations such as ladies' hair dressing. The employers thought that the men would not stand for it and refused to apprentice girls to the trade, but a chink in the defences appeared in 1868 when the men went on strike, and a Mr. Douglas of Bond Street took the opportunity of teaching a dozen women 'the great art and mystery of hair-cutting'.[22] In 1859–60 Emily Faithfull set up the Victoria Press, a venture which Munby knew but did not entirely approve of: 'Fifteen or sixteen female compositors are all the women they have on the old premises: and the actual printing, which is done here, is all done by men. The clerk in charge, whom I saw, was a man: the office boys *were* boys. This, I apprehend, is little better than trifling with the female labour question. We dont want – at least I dont – to disturb the "wages fund" by making women printers or clerks or what not: that which I want is, liberty for any woman who has the strength and the mind for it, to turn her hand to any manual employment whatever.'[23] Another project begun at about the same time was managed by Marie Rye, who established a law-copying office staffed by women. Munby used their services, but found little of real interest to him: 'To see women at such sedentary work has no charm for me. It has neither the grace and propriety of purely feminine occupation, nor the robust heartiness which makes the milkwench or the collier girl interesting.'[24]

With such idiosyncratic preferences, it is hardly surprising that Munby's views were sometimes at variance with those of other supporters of women's work such as Emily Faithfull – 'that irrepressible and inconsistent female' as he once described her.[25] He knew or had met most of the leaders of the women's movement in the 1860s and '70s – Lydia Becker (who was later to become editor of *The Women's Suffrage Journal*); Mme. Bodichon (who under her maiden name of Barbara Leigh Smith had written *Women and Work*); Emily Davies (who was foremost among those who organised the college for women at Hitchin in 1869, and became the first Mistress of Girton College, when it transferred to Cambridge); Frances Power Cobbe, 'round and fat as a Turkish Sultana, with yellow hair, and face mature and pulpy, but keen and shrewd and pleasantly humorous';[26] Bessie Parkes, 'clever hard American hatchet face she has' and on another occasion 'drest like other people for once';[27] and Elizabeth Garrett: 'She looked quite youthful and charming – one of the belles of the room: 'tis amusing, to see this learned and distinguished M.D. moving about in rosecoloured silk and pointlace, with flowers in her hair, and receiving due homage in both capacities, from the men.'[28] Social gatherings were organised at the houses of those sympathetic to the cause of women's rights, such as the radical politician Peter Taylor, Member of Parliament for Leicester for over twenty years, and Munby attended what he called 'advanced' parties, such as those in 1869 when J. S. Mill's newly published *Subjection of Women* was earnestly discussed. But he was not a wholehearted supporter of the women's movement, asking himself in his diary: 'What is all this to me, this cold and cruel crowd of doctrinaires?'[29], and it seems that he did not actively support women's suffrage.

In fact Munby felt that there were aspects of the liberation of women in society which were decidedly alarming. In 1863 he went to Caldwell's dancing rooms in Soho and met a girl who immediately attracted his attention by saying that she had come 'straight from business'. She told him that she was a copying clerk in a City office, where she worked alongside men, but was paid less than them. Munby was clearly struck by her independence, spent most of the evening talking to her, and walked her part of the way home: 'She began to express a fear lest she should "catch it"; and now the other side of the picture appeared. "I have to tell so many fibs!" said she "when I'm out late. I tell my father I've been kept at work at the office: and then he says what a shame it is to keep girls working till such hours, and why dont they put the men clerks to it? So they do, I tell him. But my mother suspects I cant be at business till eleven o'clock at night, and she dont like it at all. Many times she lets me in – for I've no latch key – and dont tell my father, else he would give it me."' If she was an example of the independent, self-sufficient girl of the future, then Munby was disturbed by the prospect. He was quite right in thinking that this girl was one of the first heralds of enormous social changes which lay ahead, and which the rules and conventions of society would be powerless to prevent: 'A young woman who is brought up to be a merchant's clerk in the city; who sits at her desk all day, and spends her evenings in going about to dancing rooms alone; who comes home late at night, and deceives her father by stories of having been kept at business: surely this is the very inversion of Nature's order – a fast "gent" in petticoats!'[30] Clearly this young woman's place is not solely 'in the home', and her very existence posed a threat to those who felt it necessary to maintain the barriers between male and female, and between ladies and working girls. She did not feel it necessary that the relationship between men and women should be regulated by those rules and 'proprieties' evolved by society to shield vulnerable young ladies who, instead of going out to work, were protected in the bosom of their family. And this 'very inversion of Nature's order' – a woman enjoying a man's freedom of action – is linked by Munby with the symbolism of dress, when he calls her 'a fast "gent" in petticoats'.

Illustration entitled *Proposed Post-Office Reform*, from *The 'Girl of the Period' Almanack for 1870.*

The 'very inversion of Nature's order' which was seen in the *Punch* cartoons revealing the possible effects of the introduction of Bloomer costume, can also be seen in this engraving of 1870 titled *Proposed Post-Office Reform*. The postwomen wear tight-fitting jackets, fashionable ankle boots, and display a shapely calf. This was published in *The 'Girl of the Period' Almanack for 1870*, and was one of a series of drawings depicting women stepping into 'men's' occupations – women lawyers, women jockeys and so on. Each was accompanied by a bogus letter which explored the humorous possibilities of the situations shown. Most of the letters purported to be written by women, but the letter which accompanied the illustration of postwomen was supposedly written by a footman. The duties of footmen – who had to be tall to be fashionable – were light, and a major part of their function was to look haughtily imposing and impress on visitors the exclusiveness of the household in possessing a servant dressed in livery. It was a common joke of the period that footmen were above carrying the coal upstairs; in this illustration by du Maurier a footman carries a letter on a tray, whilst the servant girl in front of him strains herself to lift a large scuttleful of coal up the stairs. A gentleman in such a situation would have been caught between his obligation to help a female in difficulty, and a feeling that one should not interfere with a servant merely doing her duty. Here the matter has been decided by the fact that the footman holds a higher rank as a servant than the maid. From the footman's point of view, it was a crucial question of status, and as a status symbol himself, he did not wish to harm his image. Here, then, is the letter from the fictitious footman on the impact of women's rights on the servants of a household in Belgravia in 1870:

George du Maurier, illustration for article entitled *Housekeeping in Belgravia*, in *London Society*, 1863.

Respectfully yours, Marm. — I heve acciptid office with a fust rate establishmint not fur frum Belgrave Squeeah . . . The uniform is like royal robes for splendah. But there his a droreback – there halwars his – and mine his the plaggey wimmin.

We heve six fine gals; all, except the skullry wench, lovely creeteeahs, and a cook far abuve her station, and might have wedded a cole merchint. I confess it without henvy; our fimmells at tea time make a show any hartist might feel proud to fotograf. There is also a french mamselle, a furrain nuss (*bon*), but not my sort of young woman through being too thick in the heyebrow and growing very fair whiskeah. She consorts with the house-keepah – a most objectionubble pusson, with a heye like a hork. There is also anothar gentleman, hunder me, but he is a blaggeard, and not worth talking about. To hear im sip tea is filthy. 'Hang it sar!' says I; 'ave you no hambition.' I don't think he have.

Our young wimmin air too imposing in thair harrogants. They've pisenned their-selves with some low rubbish by a party of the name of Frances B. Cobbe, and by a grand bashaw* called Stewart Mills; and they says their sects is wus than slaves. They tells a fellah to his face that wimmin is evrythink, and ornamints to the ighest perfeshuns. They hopenly calls me and the Butler tyrants and trash, and wants to know what *we* air fit for. That forwud hussy Betsey (under ouse maid), who has, I admit, a nobul countnance – after enquirin if I called myself a man, hadded that I were a fancy article from a toy shop. She have called me a poor, helpless creatuah, and offurd to carry the cole scuttle for me, lest I should get strained. I let her do so, for it *were* heavy. If she contineys obstreplus I shall put her black led brush on the best mantel piece and pack her hoff without a carracter.

I recollects the time when young gals were most civil in gentlemens cumpney, and it were a pleasuah to conwerse with cooks. I remembah when the men was expected to do

*A pasha – a high-ranking Turkish officer; used here to mean a proud, domineering man.

the courtin, and flattry was their perkeysit. I recalls the periud when, if you squeeged a gals hand, and looked her full hin the heye, she'd blush and tell you to go along. But sich times air gorn. Now the gals air that howdacius, *they* wants to be the captiwating villuns – they oguls you bold as bandits, they have a thousand trix.

Me and the Butler had a discushun with these gals the hother hevening. They begins by saying men was afraid of wimmin commin out too clevah and that was why they was snubbed and not halloud a chance. 'What more' says I '*do* yer want. Aint yer got the refreshment bars' says I 'and the pastry cook and cigar shops' says I 'and box openers and telegrarfs' says I — 'And barbers' chimes in the Butler 'for I was once shaved by a gal and never wish for a better' — 'And' I continneys 'youre printers, tailors and watchmakers, all of which' says I 'air manly follerins! what more *do* yer want' says I — That hignorant wench the scullry maid replies 'I wants to be a doctah!' — 'Well done Hannah' I cries larfing 'you allus were and allus will be a fool' says I 'you aint fit to set a saucepan to bile much less human bones' says I . . . .

St. Valentine's day being near made these gals think of postmen: yes, they'd all on 'em be postmen! They'd dress hup in the butifullest huniforms, reglar milingtary cut, quite the dandy regimental swell with nicker bocker shorts and Hungarrian boots! 'How luvly!' cries Embly, a sweet creatuah but wantin a frunt tooth. 'Wouldn't I give the double nocks and wouldn't I flirt with the footmen that hopened the door, just as that twelve o'clock delivery do with us . . . I should dearly like to break a footmans heart or make a butler jump over Waterloo Bridge, and I would too, if I was a postman!' Then she glared at us.

My blood were on the bile and the butler was spluttrin and blowin as if his steem was hup. 'You postmen!' I cries; 'you gals to be confided with bags of love letters! You do talk,' says I, 'you'd hall be transported for opening the envelopes,' says I, 'you'd steal all the wimmins hand writings from curosty and all the mens from jellesy. Hin a week you'd have to give up your lovely regmentals and put on a convics fancy costoom,' says I. 'And a very good thing it wuld be, if we culd only get rid of a pack of sarcy pussies,' says I, 'as wants to be men and wimmin at the same time,' says I, 'and aint fit to be neither,' says I.

Yours, marm, till wanted, THOS. CRANK.[31]

Munby had already discovered that England had its first postwoman in Eliza Harris of Cobham, who was unable to indulge in wearing fashionable 'Hungarian boots' as each working day she had to tramp eighteen miles over muddy country roads.

The fictitious Mr. Crank objected to the girls who wanted 'to be men and wimmin at the same time'; in real life the women workers who became the symbol of women in 'men's' jobs were the Wigan pit brow girls, who wore trousers at work. The battles fought on their behalf concentrated the attention of the public on the problems of working women. Around them raged all the arguments on the proper place of women in society, on those essential qualities which constitute femininity, and on the suitability of the 'weaker sex' undertaking hard manual labour. And Munby was closely involved in the long and emotional struggle over the pit girls' right to work.

4: A Real Social Evil?

There is a peculiarity of dress [of Wigan pit brow women], is not there? – Yes.

It is rather a man's dress that they wear, is it not? – It is rather a man's dress; and I believe, in some cases, it drowns all sense of decency betwixt men and women, they resemble one another so much.

. . .

Do you consider, from your own knowledge, that the grossest immorality takes place in consequence of the dress and occupation of the women of whom you have spoken? – I do.

Evidence given to the Select Committee on Mines in 1866
by Peter Dickinson, a miner from Aspull near Wigan.

ONE Saturday in April 1874, Munby was passing through Charing Cross Station when he 'was "struck all of a heap" by seeing in a new paper, *The Pictorial World*, a picture of Wigan wenches working at brow. What right had this artist to poach on my manor, to exhibit my heroines thus, and perhaps send people to see and spoil them, or to try and "put them down?"'[1] The front cover of this relatively new illustrated weekly newspaper carried an illustration of Wigan pit brow girls in trousers working at the coal shoots, where they removed dirt from the coal tipped from the pit wagons – *corves* in their Wigan dialect – which had come up the shaft of the coal mine. These *corves* would have been *thrutched* (pushed) across the top of the pit brow – usually by women – and *kecked* (tipped) into the shoots from above. The pit brow girls* were also employed to load railway trucks with coal, and they can be seen at work in another engraving from *The Pictorial World*. This newspaper had sent an artist to sketch the Wigan girls and was obviously hoping for some *succès de scandale* by splashing women in trousers across its front page. Munby's reaction is almost hysterical and reflects both his concern to preserve the unspoilt nature of his Wigan 'heroines', and his long battle to stop well-meaning but, as he thought, misguided philanthropists from 'putting them down'. Ten years earlier he had written bitterly in his diary criticising an article in *Once a Week* by John Plummer whom he accused of abusing the Wigan collier girls: 'I knew the abuse must come some day; but now it has

*In Lancashire they were usually called pit brow lasses, or broo wenches. Girls who did similar work in the Black Country, to the west of Birmingham, were known in their locality as pit bonk (bank) wenches, and others in South Wales, mine tip girls.

All these illustrations are taken from
The Pictorial World, 1874.

a) The front cover of *The Pictorial World* for Saturday, 18 April 1874. The illustration bears the caption *Wigan Collieries: Women Working at the Coal Shoots*. This is what struck Munby 'all of a heap' at Charing Cross Station.

b) *Wigan Colliery Girl at Work.*
This was 'drawn on the spot by our special artist' at The Mesnes Colliery, near Wigan

c) *Wigan Colliery Girl on Sunday.*

d) *Wigan Collieries: Girls Filling Trucks.*

come, it annoys me beyond expression. Am I to brave public opinion in this matter and try to show the fools that a woman may wear trousers and have coarse hands if she likes? or must we let this healthy simple labour be ended also, as other good things are daily ended? It is monstrous, the fond philosophy of these shallow philogynists [admirers of women].'[2] Plummer's article was provocatively titled 'A Real Social Evil' – the phrase 'social evil' was often used to describe the problem of prostitution – and was illustrated with an engraving of two pit brow girls titled *Mining Women in Male Attire*. He described a visit he made to a Wigan pit brow: 'Picking my way through minor piles of ashes, muddy pools, and dilapidated coal trucks, I reached the edge of the vast mass of seemingly useless rubbish, from the summit of which I beheld a spectacle utterly repugnant to my feelings, and according but ill with the character of the age. In various directions might be witnessed women with bared arms, one or two with short pipes in their mouths, performing labours totally unsuited to their sex. All were attired in male habiliments, but some had thrown aside their coats and jackets, and merely wore coarse shirts and trousers, the braces being passed, sailor fashion, over the shirts. Several of the women were using the pick, others were busy with their spades, and a few were engaged in sifting coal.' *The Pictorial World* had also instructed their artist to sketch a Wigan colliery girl in her trousers, and emphasised her man-like appearance by juxtaposing this with a sketch of the same girl wearing a dress, hat, and necklace, entitled *Wigan Colliery Girl on Sunday*. Plummer described their work as 'a species of labour which forms one of the few remaining links by which our present civilisation is united to a barbaric past.'[3]

His article was probably prompted by a paper delivered by Emily Faithfull at the Social Science Congress in 1863 on 'The Unfit Employments in which Women are Engaged'. In this she stressed that those who were trying 'to meet the wants of the age, and to open new paths for women' did not propose to encourage any kind of work which involved 'anything intrinsically detrimental to distinctive womanhood . . . We do not want to turn women into men, nor to see them doing men's work. But we go a step farther. We do not want them to be beasts of burden or unthinking machines. The loading of railway trucks, dragging coal waggons, turning heavy machines, drawing and managing boats, carrying bricks and heavy loads, are employments upon which we, at least, do not look with entire complacency.'[4] Here Munby and Miss Faithfull disagreed. He held that women should be allowed to undertake hard manual labour, provided that they wished to and did not find it beyond their strength, whilst she believed that the Wigan girls were out of place in jobs better suited to men's abilities.

Munby seems to have paid his first visit to Wigan in about 1853, when he got to know a pit brow girl called Ellen Meggison, whose nickname was 'Boompin Nelly'. She was only one of the many Wigan girls he counted

'Boompin' Nelly'. John Lancaster's Pits, from life.
Undated pen and ink sketch by Munby.

A half-naked girl dragging a loaded corf along a low mine passage; near Halifax.
An engraving used to illustrate the *First Report of the Commissioners of the Children's Employment Commission, on Mines*, published in 1842.

among his friends, and he kept in contact with her for thirty years. It is likely that Munby's attention had first been drawn to the work of women in coal mines by the *First Report of the Children's Employment Commission, on Mines* which was published in 1842 and led to Parliament passing the Coalmines Regulation Act in the same year, under the terms of which the employment of women and girls underground in coal mines was forbidden. The evidence presented in this report brought into the light of day scenes which not only exposed the cruel misuse of women and children in mines, but also revealed indecency on a staggering scale. Girls were to be seen half-naked, with their breasts exposed. One of the Sub-Commissioners reported that 'One of the most disgusting sights I have ever seen was that of young females, dressed like boys in trousers, crawling on all fours, with belts round their waists, and chains passing between their legs' as they drew loaded wagons along mine passages.[5] The Report was unusual in that it was illustrated – a new departure – and the engravings stressed both the appalling working conditions and the degradation of the women thus employed: 'This illustration of the circumstances of this degrading labour is so much more forcible than any verbal description, that we must claim permission to subjoin it.'[6] Words and images combined to put across the evidence with exceptional force. Here were girls 'dressed in boy's clothes' and 'as black as a tinker'. The Sub-Commissioner, Mr. Thomas Peace, told of Harriet Morton: 'an intelligent girl, who seemed to feel the degradation of her lot so keenly that it was quite painful to take her evidence.' No detail was spared the reader: 'The chain, passing high up between the legs of two of these girls, had worn large holes in their trousers, and any sight more disgustingly indecent or revolting can scarcely be imagined than these girls at work. No brothel can beat it.'[7] Strong words indeed. Certain elements in the Report suggest that the people it was aimed at were middle-class Londoners who knew nothing of mining. The ascents on an underground roadway in a South Staffordshire mine, for example, are described as being 'in some places steeper than Highgate-hill'.[8] And the reaction of the middle class was predictably immediate and decisive. Such work was outlawed.

Susannah Griffiths, aged 26, married Bankswoman at Caswell's pit, Wednesfield Heath, Wolverhampton. Sept. 1863. Can read & write a little.
Details noted by Munby on the back of this photograph, almost certainly taken by Marshall of Horsefield Hill.

In 1855 Munby took the trouble to search out a girl whose evidence had been quoted in the report. Ann Eggley had worked underground at Messrs. Thorpe's colliery in the West Yorkshire coalfield. Twelve years after the exclusion of women from underground working, he found her married with three children – she had been eighteen when questioned for the Report. He asked her 'Was it a good thing to turn the women out of the pits?' and she replied: 'It was for some things, but not for others. The girls never behaved badly. The work was hard, but not too hard for me. I did not dislike it, and if I was not married I'd like to work in the pit again. I'd like it better than anything else – yes, much better.' Munby notes that this was 'Statement (spontaneous) of Ann Eggley to me. She is a fine healthy woman, robust and of fair complexion and sandy hair – most respectable in appearance. All the old female colliers with whom I have conversed have expressed the same opinions and wishes.'[9] For years he collected evidence from women who had once worked underground and he seemed pleased that almost unanimously they said they would like to 'work below' again. One can only guess at Munby's motives – it is hard to believe that he wanted the 1842 Act repealed. His views on this question were decidedly eccentric. The women were not prohibited from working on the surface, at the top of the mineshafts on the pit brows. Looking back from the sixties, a subsequent Government Report stated that: 'These females, employed with the men, hardly distinguishable from them in their dress, and begrimed with dirt and smoke, are exposed to the deterioration of character arising from the loss of self-respect which can hardly fail to follow from their unfeminine occupation. It would only be a proper supplement to the measure which forbad the employment of females *in* mines, to forbid it also on the pit-banks and on the coke heaps.'[10] Certainly these girls were worked hard. Jane Harrison, an eighteen year old pit brow girl of St. Helens in Lancashire, remembered working on one occasion 'three turns together, that is, two days and a night, 36 hours, from 6 one morning to 6 the next night; never went to bed at all; had about an hour and a half in the 12, perhaps more, for meals; I only did so once; they don't often have to work more than the 12 hours on pit brow. I believe that then it was for a ship that had to leave Liverpool sooner than they thought, and wanted coaling at once.'[11]

The matter was brought to a head once more when, in 1865, the miners of Northumberland and Durham petitioned Parliament on a variety of matters including surface labour by women. They asserted 'that the practice of employing females on or about the pit banks of mines and collieries is degrading to the sex, leads to gross immorality, and stands as a foul blot on the civilisation and humanity of the kingdom.'[12] The House of Commons set up a Select Committee to look into the matters raised, and this committee sat and took evidence during 1865, 1866 and 1867. Evidence was given of the type of work done by female colliery workers, and questions were asked about the morality of the women employed on the pit banks. It was difficult for the committee members to know what line of questioning to take up in order to investigate the charges of 'degradation' and 'gross immorality'. The pit girls' dress, the nature of their work, and possible immorality seemed closely interlinked. It is interesting that one of the members asked a witness: 'Do not you recollect that the great ground for the passing of [the Act of 1842] was the ground of immorality? ... Not the hardness of the labour, but the immorality which prevailed from the exposure of the persons of women, and the indecency of it?'[13] But surface labour was considerably different, and even forceful witnesses such as William Pickard, the Miners' Agent of the Wigan District who was very much against women working on the pit brow, found it difficult to answer the question of 'what it is in this labour that degrades the women'. He replied: 'If they are employed from six o'clock in the morning to five or six at night, their absence from home leaves domestic duties entirely in a jumblement; and when the husband comes home it leads to much unpleasantness and much altercation, and leads the men to go and spend their time elsewhere.' But he agreed that this applied also to other jobs done by women. As the questioner, Mr. Woods retorted: 'I ask you what you believe to be the degradation of these women, and you answer by telling me the inconvenience caused by their labour.' When pressed further, Mr. Pickard could only reassert 'that degradation arises from their employment not allowing them to get the domestic qualifications for filling their sphere of life as satisfactorily as they ought.'[14] In effect he is saying that the place of the wife of a working man also is 'in the home', however humble.*

Considerable interest was shown in the 'peculiarity of dress' of the Wigan pit brow girls, and Peter Dickinson, a miner from Aspull near Wigan, was questioned closely on their working clothes:

As to the dress of the women, I suppose it is the most convenient dress for the kind of work that they do?

Yes.†

The entire person of the woman is covered, and there is nothing indecent in the dress, though you spoke of the dress as being one of the leading features of the degrading character of the employment?

It clothes the person, but it does not drown the feeling.[15]

*He put forward as alternative 'honourable employment' work in the mills or in service. This would have taken the women out of the home again. If his evidence appears contradictory, one should remember that his primary concern as the miners' union representative was to get the women off the pit banks, and not to solve any wider social problems. That same year – 1866 – Mr. Barton, the foreman of Barley Brook pit, near Wigan, told Munby 'that William Pickard in his evidence exceeded his instructions, and did not always speak truth. Thinks the general feeling is with the women.'

†In fact it seems that the women had worn trousers through necessity in the days when they worked underground and had simply continued to wear the same 'male' clothes, which allowed freedom of movement, when they were restricted to working above ground.

Sarah Fairhurst. Ince Hall Pits. Height 5 feet 9. Age 19. 1867 (details noted by Munby).
Carte portrait by John Cooper of Wigan.

The Select Committee, doing its best to clarify this emotive issue of the girls wearing trousers, had gone to the trouble of obtaining photographs showing pit brow girls at work, and these were used when questioning witnesses about the girls' tasks and their dress. Perhaps to counter the possible shock value of these photographs Mr. G. Gilroy, the Principal Manager of the Ince Hall Coal and Cannel Company, had sent all his pitwomen, early in 1866, to be photographed in their Sunday best by Cooper, a professional portrait photographer with a studio nearby in Wigan. When Mr. Gilroy was examined by the Committee he presented them with an album containing these portraits. The album has not survived, but this portrait of Sarah Fairhurst may be a copy of one included in it. The album was useful as a piece of propaganda to support the women's (and the company's) position, and the questioning turned not to possible immorality, but to the matter of local Sunday schools and the attendance of pitgirls at Bible classes.

Munby wrote to the Committee supporting the case for retaining women at the pit brow, spoke to members of the Committee, visited the House of Commons to hear evidence being given, and remained 'in a state of feverish mental vertigo' while they considered the matter. He was very much afraid that they would recommend that the work of his Wigan heroines be stopped.

But a new law prohibiting women from working at the pit brow would have thrown thousands of women out of work, many of whom were supporting or helping to support families with their earnings, some of them widows of miners killed in pit accidents who had taken to working on the pit banks to support their children. And so the Select Committee expressed concern through their questioning about the alternative employment which would be open to these women, as they were afraid 'that the prohibition of the employment of the vast number of women now employed in collieries and ironworks, and in other employments which are obviously unfitted for women, would be attended with a great deal of grievous suffering.'[16] It became clear that there was no significant difference between the work of the pit brow girls and that undertaken by women in other occupations which involved manual labour, for example on farms or in ironworks.

Already in 1866 a Government Report had recommended that if women were forbidden to work at the pit banks, women should also be barred from working in brickfields.[17] Brickmaking was very dirty and very laborious work. Little girls as young as eight or ten had to carry, during each day's labour, several tons of clay to the woman who worked at a bench moulding and pressing the bricks into shape before they were carried away to dry. Elihu Burritt, the American Consul in Birmingham, visited the Black Country in the mid-sixties to observe the towns and countryside in general and industrial life in particular, in order to prepare a report to send back to Washington. Here he describes the hard labour of a female bricklayer he saw at work near Halesowen:

She was a girl apparently about thirteen. Washed and well clad, and with a little sportive life in her, she would have been almost pretty in face and form. But though there was some colour in her cheeks, it was the flitting flush of exhaustion. She moved in a kind of swaying, sliding way, as if muscle and joint did not fit and act together naturally. She first took up a mass of the cold clay, weighing about twenty-five pounds, upon her head, and while balancing it there, she squatted to the heap without bending her body, and took up a mass of equal weight with both hands against her stomach, and with the two burdens walked about a rod [five or six yards] and deposited them on the moulding bench. No wonder, we thought, that the colour in her cheeks was an unhealthy flush. With a mass of cold clay held against her stomach, and bending under another on her head, for ten or twelve hours in a day, it seemed a marvel that there could be any red blood in her veins at all. How such a child could ever grow an inch in any direction after being put to this occupation, was another mystery. Certainly not an inch could be added to her stature in all the working days of her life. She could only grow at night and on Sundays.[18]

Women Brick-workers, Cradley Heath. Taken by an unidentified photographer in about 1905.

Each moulder would make about two thousand bricks every working day. The photograph of women brick-workers at Cradley Heath, close to where Burritt saw the girls at work, dates from about 1905. But their work had changed little over the intervening period; the women are working barefoot, and the clothes of the girl on the left are smeared with clay. As with the work of pit brow girls, moral objections were put forward against employing women – especially young girls – in such work: 'They become rough, foul-mouthed boys before nature has taught them that they are women. Clad in a few dirty rags, their bare legs exposed far above the knees, their hair and faces covered with mud, they learn to treat with contempt all feelings of modesty and decency.'[19] And the Rev. Mr. Dennett, who had spent three months as a missionary among the brickmakers in West Middlesex, stated that: 'It need surprise none that many in after-life should rank among the lawless, the depraved, and the dissolute.'[20]

It is difficult not to suspect that these earnest reformers, who were no doubt accurate in their descriptions of the physical work involved, were somewhat overstating their case when they cast workers in brickfields in the rôles of 'some of the most depraved and degraded characters'. 'Degraded' is a word which very often crops up in descriptions of women engaged in supposedly unsuitable work. It is usually implied that this de-grading involves a loss of femininity which also robs a woman of her place in society. A young lady would be protected at all times, either by family, friends or a chaperon; these brickyard women worked outside the ordinary rules of society, and were thus exposed to possible immorality: 'As they grow up into young women they are thrown into constant contact with young men, working, so to speak, side by side ... When there happens to be a fair, or a race, or any other amusement in the neighbourhood, they go off there together or meet there, and too often the girl's virtue is gone before her holiday is over.'[21] The fact that in eight out of ten such cases these couples got married did not make matters one iota more acceptable; such behaviour was outrageous to the morals of decent society. The very possibility of immorality by pit brow girls, brickyard women or other females open to abuse seems to have conjured up in the imagination of right-minded philanthropists scenes of sexual debauchery which more probably reflected fixed, middle-class ideas to do with the vulnerability of women and the baser instincts of men, than hard facts on outrageous and flagrant sexual assaults on women at work.

Munby told a story which pointed to the over-sensitivity of middle-class reformers on sexual matters when considering the suitability of woman's work. He was at his family home near York, and asked where Mitchell – one of the servants – was: 'I was told that he was helping Ellen the housemaid to clean windows. I enter the bathroom and find them at work. Well – there *was* a little confusion: but what of that? Similiter when Capt. A. retires with Miss B. to the conservatory, it is quite natural. But let Jack buss Jill under a hedge at fieldwork, and oh fie! It is an "unfit employment" for Jill.'[22] And even when, for example, unmarried pit brow girls had babies, there was usually more to explain the situation than an unreasoning animal passion, as Munby discovered: '"So you've got something else before you've got a husband, Ellen?" say I. "Ya, Ah've getten a lad", answered she boldly, as trying to face it out: but soon becoming subdued, she said quietly "Aye, Ah knaw it's wrang; *but they wannt marry us at onst.*" This is in fact the key of the matter: children being valuable, a woman must be proved, men think, before she is taken for good.'[23]

In 1867 the Select Committee on Mines presented its final report. Concerning the employment of women at the pit's mouth, they concluded 'that the allegations of either indecency or immorality were not established by the evidence' and therefore resolved 'that the employment of women on pit-banks does not require legislative prohibition or interference.'[24] Two years previously, in 1865, at the end of one of his Wigan visits and at the beginning of the sittings of the Select Committee, Munby had walked part of the way home with a pit brow girl: 'I said goodbye to Mary Harrison; and stood and watched her, as she walked slowly up the lane to her cottage: watched her partly for her own sake, partly because she was, as I thought, the last collierwoman I should see in the Wigan costume; in the homely decent dress of coat and flannel trousers.'[25] He must have been very pleased by the Committee's final report; their recommendation that no action should be taken meant that he was able to visit and study his Wigan heroines for over twenty years more.

There were also attempts to stop women working in other jobs involving hard manual labour. The miners' agents – that is, their union representatives – had been the most vociferous opponents of the women pit brow workers, and a similar move was made in 1882 by a Mr. Juggins, Secretary of the National United Nut and Bolt Makers Association, against women in his trade

Chainmakers' Workshops at Cradley Heath. Taken by an unidentified photographer in about 1905.

– a trade which, he claimed 'unsexed' them. The following year it was the turn of the unions to attempt to restrict the work of the female chain-makers at Cradley Heath and of women nailmakers in the Black Country. Munby had observed women nailworkers at work in their smithies near Dudley in 1863:

Some of these nailer-girls were robust and goodlooking: all were civil and quiet, and went on with their work as they talked to me. The chimney and its raised hearth are in the centre of the hut. The girl with one hand works the big blastbellows which are hung behind, and with the other pokes a long rod of iron, like a big skewer of three feet, into the cinders. Then she takes the rod out, drives the red hot end into a hole in a small anvil, snips it off above, hammers the top down into a head, and turns it out into her heap. All in a few seconds.

The girls were all about 18 or 20. They earn 1/ to 1/6 a day on an average, working from 6 a.m. to 9 p.m. 'and often longer': but it is piece work, and they can leave off when they like. . . . I think this nailmaking – the feminine form of blacksmith's work – is a capital employment for women: it is healthful; it develops their muscles and yet is not at all severe.'[26]

Only a man dazzled by a vision of female blacksmiths could call an occupation which involved considerable muscular effort for fifteen hours a day 'not at all severe'.

In 1886–7 a final attempt was made to get women off the pit brow, and the *Daily Telegraph* informed its readers that: 'An attempt is being made by labour representatives in and out of the House of Commons to have a clause inserted into the Mines' Regulations Bill prohibiting female labour at the pit's brow, and it is urged that this is being done in the interests of the women themselves, for the better encouragement of morality and as a measure of public policy.' The leader-writer went on to ask: 'Are these modern Knights of

Industry real or only pretended champions of women? Are they actuated by generous and chivalrous motives, or by what threatens to become a dangerous element in the social life of the future – the rivalry of the sexes on the broad plains of employment?'[27] All the old objections were wheeled out once again including the old line of attack about pit brow girls wearing trousers – the *Birmingham Post* commented: 'From the indignant terms in which the pit-girls' costume is denounced by some of the labour representatives, one would suppose that it was something in the nature of a ballet dress or French bathing suit, or, at least, a lady's court costume.' It also gave its opinion 'that to debar them from gaining an honest living on account of the immodesty of their attire, whilst suffering high-bred ladies to go to ball or drawing-room with the most delicate parts of their bodies fully exposed, is straining at a gnat and swallowing a camel.'[28] Another commentator noted that 'any other industry, no matter how heavy or how degrading it may be, that is performed in petticoats, is never interfered with.'[29]

Trousers were very suitable for work on the pit brow – they were warm, and they did not get caught up on moving wagons – and this new attempt to ban the workers who wore them happened to coincide with moves by the Rational Dress Society to introduce 'bifurcated garments' as sensible dress for women. How could trousers be immoral and 'bifurcated garments' be rational? The *Manchester Guardian* reminded its readers 'that, while pious hands are being held up in horror at the "disgusting" habiliment of pit girls, thoughtful and educated ladies are spending time and energy in inducing their fellow-women of all ranks to adopt a somewhat similar costume.' It then posed the very pertinent question: 'If these women were not poor and defenceless would all this disturbance have been made?'[30] The Rev. Harry Mitchell, the Vicar of Pemberton, near Wigan, and a great champion of the pit brow girls, spoke out at a meeting of over a hundred pit girls and, far from making apologies for their working attire, 'ventured to think that in twenty years' time they would be looked upon as the pioneers of civilisation in the matter of women's dress. . . . He admired their courage in wearing it, and wished there was equal courage to be found in women at the top of the social scale.'[31] A few days later the Rational Dress Society held a meeting in London open 'to ladies only' at which divided skirts were worn. It was only after greeting 'with a positive outburst of delight' the proposal that a ball should be given for showing off rational dress that these ladies acknowledged the fact that in Lancashire, irrational arguments were at that moment being used in the attempt to oust the rational dress of the pit brow girls, with one speaker 'putting in a plea for the women of Wigan'.[32]

The meetings held in and around Wigan were more rousing: 'Our cry is absolute freedom for women to earn a living within the limits of propriety, not the Mrs. Grundy propriety, but common sense propriety. You are fighting a battle for the women of England generally. Circumstances have forced me to take a lead in the matter, and knowing you as I do, there is no class of women I would sooner lead into such a battle than you. (Cheers.) I don't like to say it, for it sounds like flattery, but being a long way from home I will venture to say it. I never meet a pit brow woman who is keeping her little home together by this hard work, than my hand goes up to take off my hat to her, and only the fear that she should think I was poking fun at her prevents me. I believe your cause is now safe. So many good men and women are taking it up. (Loud cheers.)'[33] How lucky the girls were to have Harry Mitchell as their local clergyman.

Munby, by now an experienced campaigner, had already joined in the fray on the pit girls' behalf, setting forward in a letter to a newspaper his exceptional qualifications to testify for them:

I have nothing to do with mining; neither with masters nor yet with men. . . . I have explored . . . not once only, but often, all the districts in Britain where pit women are employed; and not a few districts in foreign countries also. And it so happens that I know the Lancashire pit women at least as well as I know any others. I have watched them at work hundreds of times and at scores of pits. I have sat with them at dinner time; I have walked home with them often and often, and sat down and had tea or 'baggin,'* and sat by sick beds (though I am neither parson nor doctor), and looked in on Sundays, and heard of and shared in the family joys and sorrows; and I have done this at no infrequent intervals during the lifetime of a whole generation. I could give you the names – but I will not – of many old and valued acquaintances of mine among pit women, young and old, married and unmarried; and all of these, with their husbands or fathers, have seen in me simply a person speaking their own dialect, and not unlike themselves. . . . on almost every visit I have kept a full written record, and often an artistic record too, of what I have seen and heard. And I know the result upon myself. The result is that, in my judgment, pit women, whether in Lancashire, or in Staffordshire and Shropshire, or in Wales, are amongst the noblest women that we have to boast of.'

Then he turned the question of exclusion around, and accused the accusers:

It appears to be thought right in England that a Parliament consisting of men only, should have the power of turning several thousand women† out of work and wage without their leave and against their will. That is what is meant by liberty. Let those who desire this . . . ponder this one principle: That men have just as much right, and no more, to interfere with the honest labour of woman as women have to interfere with the honest labour of men.[34]

Other supporters were more disposed to plead their cause rather than mount a counter-attack. Frances Power Cobbe wrote to *The Times* in May 1886: 'I would fain entreat members of Parliament . . . to afford the subject some reflection,‡ lest they do irrevocable wrong to their defenceless, unrep-

*Lancashire dialect for a substantial afternoon snack.
†It was estimated that about 4,500 women worked on pit brows at this time, of whom just over 1,600 worked in Lancashire. Trousers were worn only by those girls on the pit banks in the Wigan coalfield.
‡Parliament was debating the second reading of the Mines Regulation Bill.

Lancashire Pit-Brow Women.
Engraving from *The Illustrated London News*, 28 May 1887.

resented countrywomen, and drive them from their hard and rough, but honourable and cheerful toil to the workhouse, or to those darker depths where women go when they are made destitute and desperate.'[35] Most remarkably, even Emily Faithfull – who in the sixties had condemned their work as unsuitable for women – saw the light at last. In January 1886 she was still writing in support of 'the total exclusion of women from such objectionable work' and referring to the 'deadly nature of the evil'. However, 'on receiving evidence which could not be gainsaid', she admitted publicly – 'with the greatest moral courage', as another supporter commented – that she had been wrong, and was now directing her efforts to '"help" instead of "hinder" an honest class of female workers.'[36] Lydia Becker had also joined the now rather elderly band of supporters of work for women who publicly supported the pit girls' right to work. In 1866 Munby had lamented: 'No one cares for my views on women's work', and now, twenty years later, he found that the others had come round to the position which he – for his own quixotic reasons – had held for years.

It was suggested that if all else failed: 'We must try to raise a subscription for a special train to take four or five hundred of you up to London for the purpose of putting you in evidence – pit clothes and all – and of showing to the London world that you are not the degraded, unsexed, health-injured creatures depicted by your traducers, but are, on the contrary, as good an example of honourable and vigorous womanhood as England itself can produce.'[37] That was how the Rev. Harry Mitchell put forward the proposal. The newspapers preferred their more sensational version: 'London is threatened with nothing less than an invasion of colliery Amazons.'[38] This 'invasion' never took place, but in May 1887 a deputation of pit brow girls travelled from Wigan to London to see the Home Secretary, who informed them that their cause was won: 'He declined to interfere with the labour of women and girls, except in the solitary case of moving railway wagons.'[39]

When the pit brow girls marched to the Home Office, six of the twenty-two wore their working outfit – clogs, trousers, short sacking apron, topcoat and pitbonnet. It was fitting, and a tribute to his long championship of their cause, that Arthur Munby was asked to head the procession. He must have felt very proud as he lead the deputation of these 'most healthy and robust of women' through the streets of London, with Elizabeth Halliwell, the 'tallest and finest' of the Wigan pit brow girls, by his side

5: 'Honest Labour bears a lovely face.' Dekker, noted by Munby.

'Photographic portraiture is the best feature of the fine arts for the million that the ingenuity of man has yet devised. It has in this sense swept away many of the illiberal distinctions of rank and wealth, so that the poor man who possesses but a few shillings can command as perfect a lifelike portrait of his wife or child as Sir Thomas Lawrence painted for the most distinguished sovereigns of Europe.'

The Photographic News, 1861.

TODAY, anyone with a few moments to spare can take their own portrait in an automatic photo booth. In go a few coins and out comes a row of 'likenesses'. This word existed before photography, but it has a special relevance to the new breed of images produced by the camera. A photographic 'likeness' is a record of the existence of an individual. However inept the photographer, the portrait he takes records someone's mother or child or grandfather or sweetheart. So huge has been the number of photographs taken in the past century and a half, and so accustomed have we become to looking at photographic portraits, that the world revealed in photographs can even threaten to become a substitute for reality. 'My, that's a beautiful baby you have there!' exclaims an admiring friend, and the mother replies 'Oh, that's nothing – you should see his photograph!'[1] As generations pass, it

is likely that most families will be able to look back at a visual record of several generations of their ancestors with a family pride and sense of continuity which was previously available only to those who could afford to employ portrait painters to fill their walls with tangible evidence of their noble lineage. In this sense photography has a built-in democratic bias, and

Detail from a multiple portrait of babies, entitled 'Expressive Pets'.
By Hamilton Wood Jr. of London, 1874.

undermines the assumption that history consists only of a dreary procession of kings, generals and politicians. The majority of photographs celebrate 'ordinary' people – non-celebrities who otherwise live and die in comparative obscurity. Munby saw the emergence of the photographic portrait business in the 1850s and '60s and came to realise that photographic likenesses could help him to record the working women whose appearance and behaviour he tried to capture in word-pictures.

Ambrotypes by an unidentified photographer.

a) *Paper Mill Girls, Dartford, 1863.*

b) *Papermill Hand, Dartford, 1863.*

These girls worked in a papermill at Dartford. That much we know because Munby labelled the back of the photographs and gave for both the date 1863. Beyond that, nothing is known except what can be deduced from the photographs themselves and from Munby's diary entries.

The photographs are ambrotypes, which means that if you held the original in your hand you would be holding an image on a small sheet of glass about eight-by-ten centimetres. The photographer who took the portraits was no white-gloved, smartly-dressed, Regent Street 'artist photographer'. His lens seems to have been of mediocre quality – look at the falling-off of light towards the edges where the lens fails to cover the glass plate, and the image goes out of focus;[2] the chemical processing has left blobs, tide-marks and flaring which blemish the images. Much of this would have been hidden when the ambrotypes were first produced as it is likely that the glass would have been mounted in a pinchbeck frame, perhaps with a glass cover for additional protection. A century of careless handling has caused scratches and scraping.

The ambrotype was a unique image. The process used was such that duplicate prints could not be made; if you wanted another likeness, you had to take another photograph. This was because the negative produced was itself bleached and backed with black paper or coated with black varnish to produce a positive. By 1863, when these ambrotypes were made, the process was almost obsolete, and would have been found only in the studios of photographers who catered for the lower classes. The ambrotype had in the past been looked down upon as the poor man's daguerreotype. The fashionable photographers would by this date have switched to the production of *carte-de-visite* portraits – small albumen prints mounted on card – a format which had been introduced from France in the late 1850s. This was the beginning of the very rapid development of the portrait photography business, and by the mid 1860s, the number of *cartes* produced each year ran into millions. One estimate put the number of *cartes* sold annually in England at the height of the *carte-de-visite* period as three hundred to four hundred million, at a time when the population of England and Wales was just over twenty million in number.[3] Prices were low, and with the charge for a single portrait as low as a shilling or even sixpence, photography was no longer beyond the reach of the poor (a daguerreotype portrait would have cost about one guinea in the 1840s[4]) and the camera provided images of anyone and everyone from the highest to the lowest in the land. 'Who can number the legion of petty dabblers,' asked Lady Eastlake in 1857, 'who display their trays of specimens along every great thoroughfare in London, executing for our lowest servants, for one shilling, that which no money could have commanded for the Rothschild bride of twenty years ago?'[5] These photographic records of 'ordinary', unknown, unremarkable men and women are no less valuable because they were produced in their tens of thousands, or because they cost only one shilling each.

Photography was accessible – you could find a photographer's shop in your local High Street – and very matter-of-fact. Once its principles had been mastered, it was comparatively straightforward, as a commercial photographer described in 1861:

I have heard people talk about photography as if it were a very mysterious matter. I dare say that to a novice, the gradual coming out of a picture under development seems mysterious the first time or two. But it is the simplest thing in nature. It is the light and the chemicals that do it. Good light, good lens and good chemicals – these are your tools. I have seen in print a great deal of poetical nonsense about photography – waves of light, images thrown off from people and caught and retained by magic – 'quædam simulacra, modeis pallentia mireis,' (I copy that letter for letter out of a book;) 'phantoms, strangely pale' it means as they translate it underneath. You may be sure that when anyone begins to write poetically on a subject, he knows nothing of that subject. There is nothing poetical to be got out of what one knows; and every photographic artist will tell you that there is nothing in the world more plain, and matter-of-fact than photography. Whatever there is in range of your lens, you will have in your picture.[6]

Photography wasn't the end of Art, as some painters had at first thought, but its introduction and subsequent use by all classes for their own purposes overturned the notion that it was only the rich and powerful who were worthy of handing on their portrait likenesses to posterity. For every portrait of a member of the upper classes painted by a fashionable artist in the eighteenth century, there were a million and more photographic portraits of the middle and lower classes taken in the nineteenth century.

'The apparatus can't lie' was a line from Dion Boucicault's play *The Octoroon* produced in 1861, and though this is not strictly true, the camera can provide an immediacy and an intimacy with the people it portrays which enables a photograph to transcend time, allowing us to view the past directly. It would seem that the two Dartford papermill girls have decided to have their photographs taken together and sit down, hands on lap, to face the camera and remain still for the exposure. Behind them is a backdrop which hides the fact that the photograph is being taken in a fairly scruffy studio – notice the barrel on the left. The girls are not, it would seem, wearing working dress, and have done their hair carefully before the sitting. After the first plate had been exposed, the girl on the left appears to have persuaded her friend to lend her the rather smart bodice and her clean pinafore, and she sits for a second photograph wearing these and a beaded necklace. As she is a size larger than the bodice, she has to put her right hand to her stomach to prevent the fastenings bursting open and she is trying throughout the exposure to stop herself laughing – perhaps she is having to hold her breath to save herself from disaster.

By looking at these photographs we feel that we have gained some insight into the character of these girls, but we know nothing about their job in the papermill. Are they rag cutters, and does the dust affect them like the women interviewed for the Government Commission? 'I think my health has suffered: it is the dust that is bad; it hurts the chest; you have to take medicine for it.'[7] The photographs do not tell us, nor were they meant to. Photographs are often misinterpreted because they are machine-made images which seem more akin to factual records than to art. But they are far from being objective, impersonal facts comparable with, say, figures from the census tables. In 1857 Lady Eastlake described photography as the purveyor of 'facts which are neither the province of art nor of description, but of that new form of communication between man and man – neither letter, message, nor picture – which now happily fills up the space between them.'[8] These photographs demand a personal response. The girls look at the camera lens and respond by posing in order to present themselves to the future. We look back through the lens to see a girl who was alive in 1863, and who seems to be looking us straight in the eye. Perhaps we have the illusion of knowledge; perhaps the eye-contact and sense of immediacy fool us into thinking that we are somehow closer to these girls than we ever can be. Yet we have made contact of a sort over a span of a hundred years, and history seems to become living history. Photography speaks to us in the present tense; it speaks about the here and now, whether that 'here and now' is ten days, ten years, or a century ago. The messages we receive are non-verbal, and although the information may be fragmentary and out of context, the impact is immediate.

This immediacy can be a strength, and simply because the interpretation of photographs requires careful handling, they should not be set aside as a cheap, popular way into a subject – the illustrations to make the footnoted chapters speed by, the jam filling to provide flavour for the most tasteless stodge. Historians have always fought shy of the photograph; it strikes home too far and too fast. It is assumed that photographs are too often open to personal interpretation, as it is usually far from clear for what precise purpose they were taken. We do not even know, for example, who took these photographs of papermill hands. But if we can shed the accumulated sentimental, nostalgic appeal of the 'old photograph' – that sepia record of golden days gone by – and retain the down-to-earth honesty and directness of these images; and if we can then combine the visual record with the written evidence, we can begin to appreciate why Munby made a collection of photographs of working women, of which about six hundred have survived, to supplement his voluminous diary and notebook entries.

In 1859 he had written of his wish to investigate 'the moral and physical statistics of labouring women' and had for some time previously been in the habit of making sketches to illustrate his writings on working women. At best he produced quick sketches which convey the essence of a scene, for example this pen and ink drawing dating from 1855 which shows an incident on the foreshore of the Thames. A 'mudlark girl', searching for coal among the thick mud and filthy refuse, begs a bite to eat from a passing coalheaver, who gives her the remains of his dinner.

As a tireless walker of the London streets, Munby would have noticed the photographers' studios which were opening for business all over London. Early in the summer of 1861 he was out walking in Southwark: 'I passed

Mudlark Girl. Coalheaver gives her remains of his dinner. From life, Blackfriars, 1855. Pen and ink sketch by Munby.

Photographic Saloon, East End of London.
('From a Sketch'.)
An illustration from Henry Mayhew's
London Labour and the London Poor, 1861.

along Union Street, looking into strange little news shops and photographers' windows. To look on the portraits in these latter is well worth a walk through the back streets; and indeed a cento of English faces, of each class in this generation, would be valuable, and can only thus be obtained.'[9] His idea of beginning a collection of photographs to show the faces of different classes took root, and in October he returned to the same area to examine the portraits which the photographers displayed outside their studios as specimens of their work:[10] 'Most of these are of small tradesmen and their wives or young men and women of a similar class, in full fig: but now and then a working man or simple servant. I bought a few of these latter, having resolved to begin a collection of such.'[11] This is the first indication that he had taken on yet another self-imposed task, and visiting photographers' shops to buy portraits of working women – 'photograph-hunting and people-studying' as he calls it – now became a regular feature of his peregrinations.

In January 1862 he visited Winter Thompson's the photographer in Oxford Street 'who has branch shops all over the town, and might therefore have a good chance of taking portraits of working people. He tells me however, that his lowest price being a shilling, the costergirls and suchlike cannot afford to come: and as for female servants, they never come – says he – in working dress, but as smart as ever they can; often, I'm sure, they come in their mistresses' clothes: and all sorts of ways they try to hide their rough or clumsy hands.'[12] Munby was to hear this time and again, and complained that he could rarely find what he was searching for – 'portraits of working people au naturel'. What he usually found were portraits of servant girls dressed in their best clothes to have their photograph taken or, as he put it 'female servants in every stage of pretentious degradation'.[13] He bought photographs wherever and whenever he could.

When he was unable to find suitable examples it was Hannah who, as usual, had to step in and play the rôle required of her: 'I had my likeness took at this house – doing the front steps on my knees, and another shaking the mat again the area* railings – first i saw the man as i went for the beer – he was taking folks in the street, and so i let him do me wi'the jug in my hand – on glass – but these others were on cards – not done very well, but when the servants next door saw im they told their Missis, and she got them to stand in front o'their house – for her to send to India, and she gave them a card each – i was pleas'd she had them done cause it didn't look as if she thought me forward and immodest – I had mine done in my dirt to please my Massa, and they had theirn done clean'd to please their Missis only i couldn't tell them so, and they of course thought it was only to please myself.'[14] Another photograph was taken whilst she was working in Margate, after Munby had written asking her to 'have my likeness done in my dirt'. She had prepared herself by rubbing her face and arms with blacklead: 'But when i went for the pictures as he said, they wasn't $\frac{1}{2}$ so black as i was really, and i was disappointed – and Mr. S[todart] said to come out black i shd. be rubbed with *yellow*.'[15] This was because the photographic emulsions of the day were sensitive mainly to blue light, and yellow registered as black.

Hannah 'in her dirt' as a maid-of-all-work, 1864.
Carte by James Stodart of Margate.

Back in London, Munby was out once again visiting photographers in south London:

Went down by boat to London Bridge, and to my photographer's in Bermondsey: a man who looks like a retired costermonger, and who combines photography with gingerbeer and red herrings. He had got me three pictures of Bermondsey sack girls: very bad pictures, but better than nothing. 'They're the strongest wenches I could get Sir' says he: 'this here one says she can carry a hunderdweight and a alf on her ed easy'. 'I was obliged to tice em in, like' he explained 'and give em a shilling to get summat to drink; for them girls is werry pernicious about having their portraits took – they thinks it's witchcraft, or somethink o' that.' Many of them are Irish, you see.[16]

The boom in the sale of photographic portraits in the early 1860s had encouraged anybody who wanted to cash in on the craze to call themselves photographers and set to work. It was hardly surprising that Munby was disappointed by the work of this Bermondsey 'photographer' who continued to sell gingerbeer and red herrings.

Good photographs of working women were difficult enough to come by, but to find honest representations of working women in the form of paintings

Sackmaker, Bermondsey, 1862.
Ambrotype by an unidentified photographer.

*The 'area' was the yard below street level which gave access to the basement of a house, which were the servants' working quarters.

was virtually impossible. In 1859 Munby had had lunch with John Ruskin at Denmark Hill, and 'spoke to him of my favourite project – namely that some one ought to paint peasant girls and servant maids as they are – coarse and hearty and homely – and so shame the false whitehanded wenches of modern art.'[17] Ruskin 'cordially agreed' with him, but once again at the Royal Academy exhibition in the following May, Munby complained in his diary that among the exhibitors there was 'no one with courage and truth enough to paint a strong redhanded wench, and show that she may be attractive too.'[18] He had a particular, challenging subject in mind – the Paddington dustwomen resting in Hyde Park as they made their weary way homewards. 'Has any painter ever painted a group of "Dustwomen Reposing"?' he asked, and concluded that 'No painter dares to be so true to the things of common life.'[19]

'Common life' was the last thing either the artists or their patrons at the Academy exhibition would have wished to soil their hands with. To have hung a painting showing 'Dustwomen Reposing' would have been a revolutionary step in the 1860s – a subversive threat to established artists, many of whom each painted their private cloud cuckoo land for a living, and an intrusion of the real world – a glimpse of how the other half lived – which hinted at a more fundamental social and political threat to the established order.

As well as visiting the Academy, Munby also took an interest in the annual exhibition organised by the Photographic Society of London, where each year the public could review current developments in photography. Of the 1860 exhibition he wrote: 'Was on the whole much disappointed. There are many beautiful views of buildings, mountains, river and wood scenery, though these are not *better* than last year: but there is *not one* study of costume or character; not one group of English men and women – labourers, peasant-girls – to represent the dress and work and aspect of the generation. Nothing but portraits of "genteel" elegant people, such as one sees at every photographer's door; and a few made up pictures – lean ugly female models, "posed" to look like Dorotheas or Undines – if they only could! Why, the homely reality of those butcherboys, "peelers", servant maids (only these are too vain to be taken as they are) that one sees in the window of a sixpenny photographer, is better than such tawdry shams. And yet the whole life of labouring England lies open to the artist!'[20] The one photographer who had taken an interest in scenes of working life during the 1850s and '60s was Oscar Gustaf Rejlander, a Swede who had studied painting in Rome and was now a professional portrait photographer in London. As well as his day-to-day portrait work, he produced genre studies such as *All on a Washing Day*, dating from about 1854–6, for photographic exhibitions. In this the figures form a tableau displaying the various activities of the wash-house from stirring the dirty clothes by hand in a barrel of suds with a 'dolly', to pegging

All on a Washing Day.
Albumen print by O. G. Rejlander,
c. 1854–6.

out the washing to dry on the line. There is, perhaps, a hint of romantic interest as the youth glances up and hands the girl a peg. All the 'props' for this scene have been carefully assembled and the figures posed – though with a surprising lack of wooden posturing, considering that they would have had to hold their positions for several seconds. The result is only an imitation of real life, but in the mid-1850s it would have been virtually impossible to photograph real servants washing clothes in some dark outhouse. The exposure demanded would have been too long for a 'realistic' scene to be photographed, and Rejlander's painstakingly constructed piece of artifice came as near as it was possible to get to a straightforward photograph of this commonplace chore.

Munby must have seen Rejlander's studies of working people because in 1867 he arranged a photographic session with Hannah at Rejlander's studio in Malden Road, north London. Munby described Rejlander as 'a blunt but pleasant man' who 'took five pictures of [Hannah] in her working dress, indoor and outdoor, bare-armed and sleeved: and she looked as charming and picturesque, and dropt unconsciously into so many graceful poses in the sunny studio, that I would gladly have had others done, but for the cost.'[21]

Hannah as a parlourmaid.
Carte by O. G. Rejlander, 1867.

The COSTER-GIRL.
'*Apples! An 'aypenny a lot, Apples!*'
Engraving from a daguerreotype by
Beard, from Henry Mayhew's *London
Labour and the London Poor*, 1851.

The portrait reproduced here shows Hannah in the unfamiliar rôle of parlourmaid serving refreshments on a tray.[22] In real life Hannah had persuaded herself, or had been persuaded, that her duties in life were those of the maid-of-all-work: 'No Massa, i *canna* be a parlourmaid – i'm not fit, and i don't know *how* to wait at table and i always feel so awkward.'[23]

However, Rejlander's interest in street urchins, working people and incidents from everyday life was exceptional, and it was just as unlikely that a photographer would have taken a photograph of 'Dustwomen Reposing' in the 1860s as it was that a painter should think that it was a sensible subject for his talents. The photographers who sought fame through exhibition work knew that it was unlikely to be gained by photographing the poor, and most chased after their own misconception of what could be celebrated as 'photographic art'.

But the sentimental pseudo-painting which characterised much 'art photography' represented what was a trivial side issue when compared with the camera's paramount ability to record – to record everything and anything, and to record it quickly, accurately and cheaply. And the camera, everyone believed, told the truth, the whole truth and nothing but the truth – an exemplary witness.[24] It is therefore not surprising that Henry Mayhew, wishing to combine his accurate verbal descriptions with accurate visual recordings, used daguerreotypes by Richard Beard – who had opened the first professional portrait studio in Britain in 1841 – to provide some of the illustrations for *London Labour and the London Poor*.

From its infancy, photography had been used to bring back visual evidence of scenes and events which lay beyond the normal experience of most people. Photographers travelled the world, and the photographer Samuel Bourne, writing from Simla in the Himalayas in 1863, commented that 'there is now scarcely a nook or corner, a glen, a valley, or mountain, much less a country, on the face of the globe which the penetrating eye of the camera has not searched.'[25] The camera brought images of the natives of the Himalayas into the drawing rooms of those whose lives were restricted by the bounds of civilised society, and who could be shocked by scenes at the other end of the country, never mind the other end of the earth. For a fastidious London lady such as Mrs. Shaw in Mrs. Gaskell's novel *North and South* of 1854, the inhabitants of Manchester – given the name 'Milton' in the county of 'Darkshire' – were quite beyond the pale: 'Mrs. Shaw took as vehement a dislike as it was possible for one of her gentle nature to do, against Milton. It was noisy, and smoky, and the poor people whom she saw in the streets were dirty, and the rich ladies over-dressed, and not a man that she saw, high or low, had his clothes made to fit him. . . . and she . . . was afraid of one of her old attacks of nerves.'[26] And if the inhabitants of Manchester were considered 'not ones own sort', then the inhabitants of remote rural areas would seem as alien as a tribe of headhunters in Java. In the 1850s John Gregory Crace, an amateur, photographed *Irish Peasantry* and produced an image of a people who would have looked as remote to the average Londoner of the time as they do to us today. Can they really have looked like that – *Punch* caricatures of Irishmen with madonnas for wives? The camera confirms that this is indeed just how they looked – alien beings of another place, another time; as if someone had taken a photograph of peasants in the Middle Ages.

Irish Peasantry.
By John Gregory Crace, c. 1853–7,

W. Coulson, Master Sinker, and four of his men, photographed at the pit mouth, January 30th, 1862, Hartley Colliery. By W. & D. Downey. This title is incorrect. The central figure is Charles Carr, the owner of the colliery; the Coulsons, father and son, stand to his right.

And these men, who are they, and what are they wearing? They have the bearing of heroes and seem to be involved in some gigantic enterprise of engineering. Strange creatures on an unknown mission, like Victorian spacecrew waiting for the launch. In fact they are mine shaft sinkers, and this photograph was one of several taken just after the Hartley Colliery disaster by the firm of W. & D. Downey and sent to Queen Victoria. It shows the colliery owner and four experts in pit-sinking photographed at the pit mouth on 30 January 1862.[27] On 16 January, over two hundred men and boys had been entombed in a pit accident, and when rescue teams broke through six days later, they found only bodies. The grim disappointment on the faces of the men is clear to see. They are wearing suits which are too good to work in, and their shoes and clogs have been polished for the photograph. But their protective leather headgear and the capes designed to keep the water falling down the shaft from soaking them whilst they were working give them the appearance of creatures from another world.

When Dr. Johnson, that archetypal Londoner, set out on his journey to the Western Islands of Scotland in the eighteenth century he had expected to see 'a people of peculiar appearance, and a system of antiquated life'.[28] Although Munby was born just outside York, he visited the North as an outsider – a Londoner visiting the provinces. When he visited Wigan, a town which over the years he grew to know well, his attitude was that of an interested observer noting the habits of the natives. Here he reveals his feelings when leaving Wigan by the noon train on Thursday 20 August 1863:

Some 8 or 10 miles from Wigan we passed close to a pit where three strong girls were driving a railway waggon, loaded, before them by pushing with their arms and shoulders.

I looked at them with special interest; for I knew that they would be the last of the carboniferous wenches; of the trousered pea-coated Brynhilda maidens of the Wigan coalfields, who wear men's clothes without immodesty, and are strong to do men's work.

And thus I leave Wigan, as I always do, with more regret than I can avow. And yet it *might* be intelligible to some. I come hither straight from London life, and find a large town, a wide countryside, peopled *wholly* (for no others appear) with primitive working folk; no house above the rank of a pitman's cottage or petty shop; every one knowing all his neighbours simply as Jack or Mary or 'Bumpin' Nelly'; the women for once picturesquely ignorant of fashion, even on Sundays, and strolling about the main streets not only in quaint old costume, but actually – such is their Japanese innocence – in men's clothes: I go and live in rude dress among this race; chatting with rough hearty men, rough hearty wenches; treated by all as an equal; hearing their broad salient speech, and speaking it too as far as I can do so: why, 'tis a new world. And if completeness of relief be gauged by intensity of contrast, then I may well enjoy such a world – after London![29]

Once again one can tell how Munby needed his experiences in London society to contrast with the life of these 'primitive working folk'. He was just as anxious to obtain photographs of these 'Brynhilda maidens' as he had been to collect ambrotypes of working girls in London, and once again he did not find it easy to get the photographs he wanted.

Today, when an automatic camera will produce finished prints almost immediately, and anyone can become a reasonably competent photographer, the idea of having to entice people into the nearest available portrait studio in order to obtain a photograph of them is ludicrous. A century ago the foolproof snapshot camera with its reassuring slogan 'You press the button, we do the rest'* lay in the future, but even considering the difficulties to be overcome, Munby would have gained enormously by learning how to take photographs himself.

It is unlikely, however, that Munby took a single photograph in his life. There is a tantalising diary entry for 9 November 1863: 'To M'Lean, Haymarket† – Camera £6.6.0'.[30] Had it crossed Munby's mind that he should take up photography and was he investigating the cost? His diaries do not tell us. It would have been a sensible step to take, and would have meant

*George Eastman's slogan for his hand-held Kodak camera, introduced in 1888.
†McLean & Haes, photographers and miniature painters of 26 Haymarket, from whom Munby commissioned portraits of milkwomen in the following year.

that he could have broken free from his reliance on professional portrait photographers and produced much less impersonal results than some of the *carte* portraits he bought. There would have been no need for him to sort through the old stock and specimen prints of semi-competent backstreet photographers and be satisfied with whatever he came upon by chance. The wet-plate process which he would have had to master was quite difficult and messy, however, and the equipment required, including a portable darkroom for work away from home, was bulky and heavy. One amateur who overcame these difficulties was Lewis Harding, who photographed the fishing community of Polperro in Cornwall during the 1860s and '70s.[31] His portrait of the two fishergirls knitting guernseys dating from about 1860 displays an intimacy and liveliness which is usually missing from the rather stiff formal portraits which Munby was able to collect. The sort of photographs Munby would no doubt have liked to have taken were simply beyond the technical limits of the cameras of his day. Even when the wet-plate had been replaced

by the much faster dry-plate process, exposure times were not short enough to stop action at close quarters, as the photograph of the street scene in south London in 1884 shows. The matchseller, the woman with a basket of apples and the sandwich-board man have remained still for long enough to register clearly on the plate, but a figure on the left of the photograph, perhaps twirling a cane, has moved and blurred so much as to be almost invisible. Similarly, the passing horse-drawn traffic becomes almost indecipherable, and a phantom foot on the right indicates another moving pedestrian. The generation of hand-held cameras heralded by the introduction of the first Kodak in 1888 brought the era of the snapshot and

Polperro fishergirls knitting Guernseys, *c.* 1860.
By Lewis Harding of Polperro, Cornwall.

Apples, Matches, Sandwiches.
Taken in Borough High Street, London by R. L. Sims in 1884.

Four girls laughing.
Taken in 1905 by Frank Clarke, the
brother-in-law of Mrs. Pankhurst.

did away with the need to process your own plates and prints. The intimacy
we begin to feel when Munby is describing whole days spent on Wigan pit
brows talking to the girls who worked there, finds a visual form in
photographs such as *Four girls laughing*, a snapshot of Manchester working
girls taken in 1905 by Frank Randall Clarke, the brother-in-law of Mrs.
Emmeline Pankhurst.

Compared with this, the *carte* portraits of pit brow girls which he was able
to buy from professional portrait photographers in Wigan are lifeless and
formal. Many of the visual qualities of these photographs result from force of
circumstance. The girls have been asked to come to the studio and to wear
their working dress. They are provided with suitable emblems of their tasks at
the pit brow – sieves, spades and lumps of coal* – posed, with the back of their
neck against a metal headrest, and finally, no doubt, asked to 'look natural'.
The fact that they do not look natural in most of the *cartes* collected by Munby
is hardly surprising.

*Robert Little, one of the photographers from whom Munby bought *carte* portraits, had a spade
which can easily be identified in his photographs as it is worn down and has a piece missing.

Ann Fairhurst, Ince Hall Pits, 1868 (noted by Munby).
Carte by John Cooper of Wigan.

Wench from Ince Hall pits – age 30. Background inserted at her own request. 1863 (noted by Munby), *Carte* by Robert Little of Wigan*.

Shevington, 1867 (noted by Munby). *Carte* of pit brow girls standing by a coal truck, by T. G. Dugdale of Wigan.

These are three examples from his collection. The first is so straightforward and lacking in artifice that it looks modern – the record of some social anthropologist or the work of a twentieth-century photographer who has seen the work of August Sander, or perhaps Lewis Hine. The second is firmly rooted in the conventions of nineteenth-century portrait photography. Munby noted on the back of this *carte* that the painted background was inserted at the girl's request. The bizarre juxtaposition of a pit brow girl holding in her hands the symbols of her work – a sieve and a spade – standing against a backdrop of a terrace supposedly overlooking a romantic lakeland scene, and at the same time standing on a floor covering of striking design is bewilderingly surreal. The third was taken outdoors at Shevington in 1867 and shows two girls leaning back against a coal truck. The camera and a portable darkroom would have had to be carried to the pit brow in this case, and the special effort required to obtain this photograph may indicate that it was commissioned specially by Munby.

What these photographs lack in the way of sophistication they make up for in their directness. There are no frills – no concern about camera angles or close-ups, no dramatic lighting, no searching for a pose which will provide some expressive gesture or indication of character. These are machine-made images, and they have their origins in the camera and not in any tradition of

*Robert Little's name appears on the *carte* mounts, but Munby's description of the studio in Clarence Yard reveals that often it was Mrs. Little who actually took the photographs.

a

Photographs by Dr. Edward Dingley
taken in Wednesbury *c.* 1890.

a) Titled *Coal Picking*, showing children
playing in the gutter.

b) *Colliers, Blue Fly Pit, Ridding Lane.*

c) *Pit Bank Wenches, Blue Fly Pit.*

b

painting. They are straightforward to the point of bluntness, anonymous photographs in which the only part the photographer plays is that of camera operator.

These photographs of the Wigan girls were precious mementos of his Northern heroines, to be admired on cold winter evenings when he sat at home in London in front of a cheering fire – a fire which burned Wigan coal: 'I have just got a ton of Kirkless Hall coals, for the sake of my Wigan friends. Every skuttleful I now use, was brought from the pit's mouth, and placed in the railway trucks, by women; and women, too, whom I have seen and known, heartily working away in their suitable jackets and trousers. Mysterious bond of sympathy! This big lump of coal, which I daintily put on with the tongs, has lain, perhaps, in the broad black hand of Jane Brown or of Bumping Nelly! Every lump has thus its individuality, its history; and I cannot mend the fire without being reminded of days spent with those brave rough lasses of the north, on their pit broos and by their rude cabin fires.'[32] The photographs were part of the set of symbols he surrounded himself with to remind him of labouring women; Hannah – 'my sweet wife, in her servant's dress, and looking lovely in her Filey fishwoman's bonnet'[33] – also played her part in this.

It is when you look at photographs taken by others interested in working class life that you can appreciate how exclusively Munby concentrated his attention on working women. The photographs showing pit bank wenches at the Blue Fly Pit, colliers in the cage at the surface, and children playing in the gutter were taken in about 1890 at Wednesbury in the Black Country by Edward Dingley, a local doctor. Dr. Dingley no doubt had his own personal

c

interests – his motives for taking these photographs are not known – but he provides an over-all view of the mining community – men, women and children. Munby would have been interested solely in the pit bank wenches. The men and children would only have been worth noticing as the husbands or offspring of the working women.

It may be that Munby took the decision *not* to become a photographer and actually enjoyed visiting the shops of photographers who catered for the lower classes, and inveigling girls in to pose for their portrait. Taking a photograph might have seemed to him a rather tiresome chore; it was much more exciting to pluck a specimen off the streets. As both painters and photographers were averse to picturing his proposed 'Dustwomen Reposing', he determined to capture the likeness of one of them for himself. These dustyard girls worked hard for as many as ten hours a day, and were not the most easy creatures to entice into a portrait studio. Munby described gangs of them crossing Hyde Park on their way home 'bearing down upon one, gaunt and gigantic with creel on head, like Birnam Wood on its way to Dunsinane.'[34] He also saw two of them fighting their way out of the midst of a crowd gathered to watch a military review – a crowd in which they had got stuck: 'The taller of the two lasses went first, squared her shoulders, brought her right elbow well forward, steadied her creel with her left hand; and then threw herself upon the people next her, shouting "Now then – clear the way, cripples!" And the cripples did clear the way; they fell back before the two Cinderellas as before a chimneysweep; and the strength and dirt and rags of the maidens carried them off in triumph.'[35]

Here then was a challenge for Munby, and he became embroiled in all manner of unexpected complications when he set out to get a photograph of a dustgirl taken for him by a photographer called F. Lindsey of Lambeth:

I crossed Westminster Bridge by the temporary wooden footway; at the Surrey end of which I found a group of dustwomen, resting on their way home. They were leaning against the parapet, on which they had placed the large creels of refuse that they carry on their heads. It occurred to me that this was a good chance of obtaining a photograph of a woman of this class in working dress. Knowing however that the creatures would be simply astonied if I made such a request in person, I asked a photographer's doorsman close by, if he could persuade one of the women, whom I pointed out, to come and be taken. He went off to do so, and returned to the door with her: but seeing me, she quickly ran away again. 'She's a stoopid!' cried the doorsman; and rushing off once more, he brought her back; and grinning and wondering, she tramped up stairs like a ploughman. I followed; and in a little room that served as showroom and parlour, I found the photographers, two respectable young men, and two girls, their sisters apparently, who were seated at needlework. The dustwench, all in dirt as she was, had plumped herself down in a chair by the door, and sat silently staring: and the disgust and astonishment with which the two milliners looked at their coarse masculine sister, was very amusing. Rapidly noting the contrast, but speaking as if the whole affair were a matter of course, I said to the young men – who had preserved an air of businesslike indifference to my fair friend –

Dust Girl, Lambeth Yards, 1862.
Ambrotype by F. Lindsey of Lambeth.

'Can you take me a portrait of this woman?' They agreed; and 'this woman' was marched on up to the glass house.

She was a stout rough Irish lass of two and twenty, with big muddy boots and a ragged cotton frock looped up over a grey kirtle; her neck and chest protected by a thick brown kerchief. Her arms, which were strong and full, were bare; but she carried a man's heavy corduroy jacket over her shoulder – a filthy thing, black with coaldust. Indeed, as she was fresh from ten hours of work among the dust and cinder heaps, her clothes and arms and face and hair – which her battered bonnet left uncovered – were all smeared and powdered to a dull dingy blackness. She put on her jacket at my desire, and sat down, holding her tin dinner-can before her: and when I had posed her thus – which I did with my gloves on, seeing how dirty she was – the lens was uncovered.

They kept her several minutes, for the light was very bad; and wonderfully still she sat, not moving even her eyelids. But when it was over, she drew a long breath and said 'Eh! Well, that *is* a punishment! that's wuss than a day's work, that is.' 'What,' said I, 'worse than a whole day in the dustyard?' 'Aye, that is it' she said; 'sitting still like that and niver movin' – why, my eyes is full o' watter!' So they were, indeed; and she took out a tattered handkerchief (an unusual luxury!) and rubbed them; wiping off as she did so some of the many strata of dust upon her face.

A second picture was taken of her by the photographer for his own satisfaction; and then 'Now I think we may dismiss her' I said. She understood me, and quickly exclaimed 'Ain't you a goin to give me nothin Sir?' and then, having received a shilling, she huddled up her things, tramped downstairs in her rude manlike way, and exit. . . .

I came away when the picture was ready; leaving behind me, as I thought, no other impression than that of wonder at my bad

taste, in desiring to possess the portrait of a clumsy dustwoman rather than of (say) an elegant young milliner in costume of the period. But, as I gave the doorsman a fee for his trouble, he remarked that he had 'another young woman' close at hand – 'a beautiful specimen'. I asked what he meant; and by way of reply, he plunged into a publichouse next door, and produced in a twinkling the damsel in question, who had evidently been in waiting: a tall palefaced girl in mourning of fashionable make though somewhat shabby. He set her before me in the passage, adding by way of introduction 'She's an envelope maker Sir – there's lots of 'em hereabouts.' The girl looked quiet and modest; and what I was expected to do with her I could not conceive. I passed on therefore, simply telling her that she was not the sort of hardworking person whose portrait I wanted. The doorsman however came forward and whispered that he had brought her 'to have a picture of her taken *with her clothes up*'. Here was a revelation indeed! The fellow, finding quickly enough that he had made a mistake, took to vehement apologies – 'he was an old soldier' (he wore a medal) 'and no doubt I was an officer – and he thought etc. – and he meant no harm.' I walked off in disgust; but the scene was not yet over. A shabby-genteel young man who had been lingering about now came up to me bowing. 'beg pardon Sir – but was you in want of any ballet girls or poses plastiques?' I stared and answered No: but, reflecting that fas est [et] ab hoste doceri,* I added 'what have you to do with such matters?' 'Sir,' replied the seedy one 'I am a theatrical agent: I can supply you Sir with girls, for ballet or poses or artists models, at an hour's notice, if you honour me with an order.'

And he offered me a dirty envelope containing his address.

I thanked him coldly, and so got away at last; wondering why on earth a dustwoman's

*'It is right to learn even from our enemy.' Ovid, *Metamorphoses*, IV, 428.

portrait should have produced these offensive results. There had been no appearance of evil in the matter; the photographer seemed respectable; and I can only conjecture that Astley's theatre, and the crowds of mean workgirls who live thereabouts, may have been local causes for the annoyance. One may suspect too from this incident, that a good deal of Holywell Street photographing goes on in places which are outwardly respectable.

And off he went to a social gathering where he saw Millais and Holman Hunt, who 'cordially shook hands, though I know him but slightly.'[36] Munby was able to cram a very wide range of experience into a single day.

A few weeks after the incident with the dustgirl his motives were again misinterpreted and he was accosted once more:

A 'Photo. Tout' outside a 'Photographic Saloon' accosting a passer-by.
Detail from a *Punch* cartoon of 1871.

Going into a small photographer's shop on my way home, to buy a beautiful view of the Haunted House at Hampstead, the man, who was young and well drest, wanted to show me various photographs of nude female figures. Producing one, of a young woman *entirely* naked, 'This Sir,' said he 'is Miss Peacock, the Academy model'! . . . I did not look at the others, except one, which struck me by the strange contrast it exhibited: for it was the picture of two very respectable damsels, fully clothed, but holding up their dresses in a grossly indecent manner. I enquired how persons of such modest aspect came to sit to a photographer in such a fashion. 'Oh,' said the man, 'there are many of them do it in the daytime. They come of their own accord – I've known quite a lot of girls come to us as early as six o'clock on a Sunday morning; for Sunday's the best day for them. Give them something to drink, and they dont mind how they are taken, nor in what postures, however degrading.[37]

The Society for the Suppression of Vice went on the offensive in sending agents into photographers' shops in Holywell Street and in other parts of London to suppress this trade. An agent ran to ground a wholesale dealer in Long Acre in 1870. The premises of Henry Evans were searched by a detective, and eight hundred and fifty obscene photographs seized. At the trial, the judge said that 'he should not waste many observations upon a person like the prisoner at the bar, for he knew that these infamous articles were sent by post, and in some cases they were thrown over the walls of ladies' boarding-schools, and there was no limit to the evil that might be caused by them.'[38] Evans got two years hard labour and a fine of fifty pounds.

It must have crossed the minds of the working girls Munby enticed into photographers' studios that perhaps they were in for more than a photographic session. Munby found many – especially those who did not know him – who refused either because of their own fears, or their fears of what their husbands or sweethearts might say. Parents, too, could be difficult; the father of a girl who worked on a farm refused to let Munby have a photograph taken of her: 'he wouldn't have nothing o' the sort: *he* wouldn't have the girl made a laughing stock of.'[39]

Munby saw the dustgirl whose photograph had been taken on one other occasion. Almost a year later, he saw her in the street, and remembered her:

In crossing Westminster Bridge I saw a rough clumsy young woman running towards me at full speed, keeping the kennel [the street gutter] to avoid the crowd on the flags. . . . I recognised her as the same girl whose photograph I had taken last year, and who thought that sitting five minutes to be photographed was far worse than her day's work at the dustyard. The welldrest men and women turned round with disgust to look at this wild creature, plunging along at the top of her speed, with her great uncomely limbs flung all abroad as she ran.

Suddenly in her haste she dashed against the wheels of a passing hansom. Flinging up her black hands she recovered herself with a howl of surprise; the driver meanwhile in contemptuous frolic lashed her with his whip; but she took no notice of the indignity, and continued running; diving into the throng of vehicles that filled the broad road, she disappeared.[40]

It is typical that Munby should record this trivial and insignificant incident. It tells us nothing about the dustyard business, but a great deal about Munby's attitude to the working women he observed.

This glimpse of a dustgirl, like the decaying photograph of her, is of an individual pulled by Munby out of the crowd. A person of no significance to society, she is valued by Munby, who tried to come to terms with the vast toiling armies of women workers in London – and elsewhere – by observing those that he happened upon in daily life, and, by securing their individual likenesses in words and in photographic portraits, hoped to record them for posterity.

II: PORTRAITS FROM LIFE

IN this section of the book I have tried to convey the sense of excitement and deep personal involvement to be found in Munby's descriptions of working women in his diaries and notebooks. These word-pictures of the girls he met are vivid and often touching, and his collection of photographs – an added bonus to these outstanding descriptions – plays an integral part in recreating, for example, his meetings in the London streets with milkwomen, and those glorious days when he braved the swirling coaldust and the salt sea spray to talk to his heroines of Wigan and Filey. The photographs which he took so much trouble to search out, and the ambrotype and *carte* portraits which he cajoled and pestered working girls to sit for, both complement the vividness and immediacy of the diary entries and are set firmly in context by them. This precise 'placing' of these photographs by Munby's written evidence makes his collection exceptional; the photographs of working women are located by him in their place as pieces of social history, and function both as documentary records and striking visual images – arcane mysteries of a private world of interest.* His words and photographs together do not produce a complete portrait of the labouring women he devoted his time and energies to studying, but they offer a unique opportunity to see through the eyes of a devotee and *amateur* at least a partial picture of the sort of women they were, and the life that they led.

I have used extracts from Hannah Cullwick's diaries to stand in for the lack of descriptions by Munby of the everyday humdrum tasks of the maid-of-all-work. Her extensive diaries would repay much further study and provide both a poignant record of her love for 'Massa' and a very shrewd and observant view of her 'betters' by a woman who was the lowliest servant in a London household.

Pit brow girl.
Undated pen and ink sketch by Munby.

*Almost all the photographs reproduced here are from Munby's collection (those from other sources are indicated by the prefix □). The italicised parts of the captions are transcribed from Munby's own notes which he made on the back of the original photographs.

*Ellen Grounds, aged 22, a broo wench at
Pearson and Knowles's Pits, Wigan, taken
11 September 1873.*
Munby stood beside her 'to show how
nearly she approached me in size'.
Carte by Robert Little of Wigan.

1: Wigan Pit Brow Girls

Wigan – 'the picturesque headquarters of rough female labour' Munby, describing the town in his diary.

Friday 19 August 1859. Got out of the train at Hindley, where the Wigan coal district begins. The first pits I came to were of the Kirkless Hall group – three close together, and about a quarter of a mile from the station. Those black nondescript creatures pushing the waggons along the embankments would not be noticed by travellers on the line: they would pass for men; but I recognised them at once as my stout hearty friends, the Lancashire colliergirls. The costume of these girls and women is always the same, and a good useful one it is. A hooded bonnet of padded cotton,* pink blue or black; a blue striped shirt, open at the breast; a waistcoat of cloth, generally double-breasted, but ragged and patched throughout; fustian or corduroy or sometimes blackcloth trousers, patched with all possible materials except the original one; and stout clog shoon, brassclasped, on their bare feet: round the waist is tucked a petticoat of striped cotton, blue and black, rolled up as a joiner rolls his apron; it is never let down, and is perfectly useless   only retained as a symbol of sex. At the first of the three pits I found four women, all young: one was standing with her hands in her pockets, and another sitting dangling her legs on the edge of a railway coal truck, waiting for coals from the pit's mouth to fill it. The third girl I found behind a great bank of coke, digging it down with a spade ready for the corves. While talking to her, a train of empty corves started down the slope towards us from the pitsmouth: the fourth girl who was in charge of it, took a flying leap, as she set the train a

going, and stuck on to one of the corves till they reached the bottom where we were; then jumped off, and straightway seized her spade and fell to digging without a word. She was a pretty brunette of eighteen, strong and healthy: her clothes, even her coarse flannel trousers, were in good condition; and dirty as she was, she had been woman enough to stick a bunch of halfripe wild cherries in the side of her grimy bonnet.

Saturday 29 September 1860. I went to a neat row of stone cottages just beyond Frank Holme's [a public house at Springs Bridge, near Wigan] and knocked at the door, which stood open, of the centre one. I went in, and found a room comfortable in a rough way, but untidy, it being cleaning night. Before the blazing fire sat a boy, grimy and in pit clothes, resting after his work; and a bony sallow girl from a factory was eating her supper at the dresser. These were Jane's brother and sister. Her mother came in directly; a stout loud-voiced woman, hot tempered evidently, but goodhumoured and kindly in a blunt fashion; comely also, and neat enough. She asked me to sit down; I explained about the picture [he had come to buy a photograph of Jane in her trousers] and she was going to produce it, when shouts and trampling of clog shoon were heard outside, the door was driven open, and in burst the two wenches, Ellen Meggison and Jane, shouting and tumbling over one another like lads at a fair. They were both of course in their pitclothes, and as black as ever; and their grimy faces were bathed in

*Munby later noted that the hoodbonnet of the nearby St. Helens pit girls 'differs from the Wigan one in having – strange finery for a pitgirl – a *feather* in front.'

□ *Pit brow girls at work, 1898.*
Carbon print by Thomas Taylor of Platt Bridge, near Wigan. Note the comparative sophistication of this pit head – photographed at the end of the century – with safety gates at the mouth of the mine shaft, gas lighting, and with a range of mechanical wagon-tippers and other devices to aid efficiency.

Jaan Brahn (Jane Brown) pit brow girl.
Carte by John Cooper of Wigan.

Jane Brown, Bottom Place Pit.
Carte by John Cooper of Wigan.

sweat, for they had been running home all the way. The mother instantly began to rate Jane soundly for staying at the alehouse and being out so late (it was now 7.30): 'is that the way for a respectable young woman?' thundered she – evidently not merely because *I* was present. The girls shouted in reply that they had had to do overwork and to wait for their wages: and the hubbub subsided, and Ellen flung herself into a chair, and Jane leaned against the drawers, panting, and wiping the beaded sweat – and with it some of the blackness – from her red face, with the end of her neckchief. It was a singular group – the quiet coaly boy by the fire, the sallow pale sister and stout clean mother, and then those two young women in men's clothes, as black and grim as fiends and as rough and uncouth in manners as a bargee, and yet, to those who looked deep enough, not unwomanly nor degraded. They soon became

quiet, after the first burst: and their talk had nothing flippant or immodest in it. Jane sat down to her supper of Irish stew; scooping the potatoes out of the bowl with a leaden spoon, and holding the meat in her black fingers while she tore it from the bone with her teeth. Her mother and I meanwhile stood and looked at her – she eating away unconcerned and hungry – and remarked what a fine healthy wench she was, and how she was not seventeen till next month, and so on. And yet this colliergirl of seventeen is ten times more robust and womanly than her elder sister the factory girl. . . . At last I had the picture (which was not a good one) produced, gave Jane the shilling for it, and sixpence to Ellen for 'a gill o'yal' [ale] and said goodnight . . . here I am sorry to admit that as I left the cottage, Ellen started up and ran after me, dragging Jane with her, to beg that I would come into Frank Holme's and treat them to some *gin*. When I flatly refused, however, they both retired quietly, saying goodnight; Ellen going home to her grandmother's cottage further on.

Tuesday 18 August 1863. I reached the high road from S. Helen's to Ashton and Wigan, at a small collierhamlet named Black Brook. Going up the hill through this, I came, just beyond, to the first of the Haydock pits, which extend for a mile or more towards Ashton. As I neared it, the usual train of coaltrucks was standing under the shoot; and upon one of them a figure with a shovel in hand was busy loading.

It was a woman wearing trousers: the first I had met with today. They told me at Laffak that the Haydock pits are the nearest to S. Helen's of all those where this Wigan costume prevails: and so it was. Black Brook is a Rubicon which no pitwench in 'breeches' may pass. From this first pit I could see the canal quay, with its female workers, only 200 or 300 yards off: yet those women 'reckoned they'd be shaamed' to dress thus, while these walked about in their trousers with utmost indifference – and, I may add, with not less modesty than the others in their kirtles [skirts].

I wanted to find out *where* the change of dress took place, and *why*: but to the second question the only reply is, Custom. From here for 8 miles on to Wigan, and thenceforward again for 8 or 10 miles more, the collier-wenches universally wear breeches: which, as the sturdy old banksman at this Haydock pit assured me, are better and more comfortable than petticoats. . . .

Only for my luggage, I should have walked on from hence to Wigan: but as it was, I contented myself with having solved the Great Breeches Question, and walked smartly back to S. Helen's by the road, arriving just in time for the 4.30 train.

Wednesday 19. I went out soon after nine, to Dugdale the photographer. Found he had

Jane Horton, 19, Kirkless Hall Pits, Middle Patricroft. Wigan Aug. 1863. (formerly a factory girl.)
Carte by T. G. Dugdale of Wigan.

Pit brow girls, *1868.*
Carte by Robert Little of Wigan.

lately taken a good picture of one Jane Horton, aged 19, a collier at Patricroft (Ince Hall) and formerly a factory girl. She was a niece of Dugdale's next door neighbours, a very respectable woman, who offered to send for her at once, if I liked. Apropos: I saw this and one or two other 'cartes de visite' of girls in pit clothes hung up in the street by the photographers; one of whom in Clarence Yard told me they often come to her to be taken thus clad, and rather like to be exhibited.

Friday 17 March 1865. Fine sunny morning: afterwards cold and cloudy, with keen east wind. I went out at nine to the photographers: to Dugdale, who has at length taken a group of pit wenches at a colliery near Telure's, toward Gathurst to Cooper,

Walsh Nan. 1867.
Carte by Robert Little of Wigan.

who sells beer as well as photos, and who said he had sold hundreds of cartes de visite of the collier girls, who already had told me the same story: and to Little, an inferior party near the station. A case of his photos hung on view in the main street, and among them were several portraits of pitgirls in costume. As I looked at them, two young women in female clothes and with shawls over their heads came up and looked also. 'Why,' said one 'yon's Walsh Mary Ann!' and so it was; Ann Morgan of Hindley. 'And that,' she went on, pointing to a picture of a fine comely lass in loose shirt 'is Jane Underwood, that worked at Pigeon Pit; and that' – a goodlooking robust woman leaning on a spade – 'is King's greaser; Mary they called her; she greases the railway-truck wheels.' So you have worked on pit-brow? I asked. 'Aye, many a year!' said the girl. Just then an Officious Party, one of a small crowd which had gathered round, thought it well to explain what those trousered figures were. 'Them's *women*', he said 'they're not men'. Men, indeed!

All the four photographers said they sold these photos chiefly to commercial travellers, who buy them as 'curiosities'.* 'Many strangers passes their remarks upon 'em,' said Mrs. Little; 'and some considers as it's a shame for women to wear breeches, and some takes it for a joke, like.' Just so: some are sentimentalists, some sensualists: none rational and serious.

. . . I left Wigan on foot at 11.45, to walk to S. Helen's and see the pits en route. . . . .

I was now about 6 miles from S. Helen's and it was 2.30 p.m. – A respectable old man at the coal office on the brow advised me not to go by Billinge, which lay out of sight to the right: there are pits that way, said he, but more if you go the longer route by Blackleyhurst: such as those yonder, of Sammy Stock's. So I took his advice. . . .

Going thence down the line, I came to a siding, running up to the next pit, No. 3. Here in the cutting I found a girl lounging about with her hands in her breeches-pockets, whistling. She turned out to be the pointswoman, whose duty it is to mind the rails whenever a train of coalwaggons goes by. I was struck by her brisk and easy air, and stopped to talk with her, and she seemed glad enough to have some one to talk to. Her name was *Margaret Roughley*, and her age 17; she has a elder sister working on the pit brow close by. This Margaret was a wellgrown girl: her collier bonnet was tilted over her eyes, which sparkled under lashes thickly clogged with coal dust: her face was very black, but also singularly expressive and intelligent: her arms were bare: she had a woollen comforter round her neck; a loose patched shirt, looking very thin and cold; a short baglike apron of sackcloth; short fustian trousers, only reaching to the calf; grey stockings, and big clog shoon, whose iron soles were turned up at the toe like a Chinaman's boot. Had she no coat? I asked: it must be very cold, waiting about in this cutting all day. No, she had not: but the Gaffer's very kind – he lends me his coat when it rains: and besides, she said, Aw don't stop here all day; Aw'us waggons to fill wi' slack; 20 waggons a day sometimes; yo'd not think it was idling if yo'd got *that* to do! And Margaret laughed a boyish laugh, and showed her white teeth, like Irish diamonds set in black bog oak. Then, as there were no trains coming, she leaned her back against the earth of the cutting, crossed her legs easily, tucked her hands under her 'barmskin',† and looking straight at me, talked away for ten minutes as gaily and freely as if she had always known me. She spoke the broadest Lancashire, and spoke it so fast that I could scarce follow her: e.g. 'Aw'd goo'sairce'moo'r lemma', = service if mother'd let me. She didn't dislike this work, however; and though

Cartes of Wigan pit brow girls in their trousers could also be bought at W. W. Wilding the tobacconist's in Standishgate, Wigan, and were to be found on sale as far away as Manchester.
†An apron, usually of leather.

now she only earned 1/- a day while the broo-wenches earn 1s/2d, she hoped soon to be 'raised', and she had been 'raised' from 10d. a day already. She could not read; yet she was one of the brightest and most interesting girls I ever saw: as sharp and lively as a London street boy, yet with nothing impudent or unfeminine about her. True, her dress and manners were those of a lad; she jumped and ran, and hitched up her trousers, like one who knew nothing of petticoats; but in all her words and ways there was an artless simplicity and trustful frankness that was thoroughly girlish. She had humour, too, and wit beyond her years; she was always saying something comic and then merrily laughing at her own conceit: she laughed at her grotesque attire: 'such queer old clothes as we wear!' said she 'ragged ones that folks gie us – our brothers' old coats and breeches – anything does to work at pit in; but we wear our breeches always, yo know, 'cept Sundays – and nice and warm they are too!' and she threw her left leg over her right as she spoke. 'Eh!' she went on 'bud yo *will* laugh at thoose wenchcs at Two pit – they're all such rags – ho ho!' and she laughed again. Strange creature . . . a black ignorant colliergirl of seventeen, in breeches and clogshoon, and yet winning and loveable, and clever enough to repay a deal of teaching.

When I said I was going to see the other wenches 'Aw'll coom wi' ye' she cried, start-ing up 'and see hah they're gettin' on' – and we went. On the way, she remarked that she would look queer if she were 'drawed aht' just as she was. Why, did you never see them done? I asked. No, she said – Why, they wouldn't do it, would they? To be sure they would, said I, and straightway showed her one of my Wigan photos. The girl stared at it a moment and then shouted aloud with won-der and delight, and insisted on taking the picture into her black fingers, pleading that she wouldn't hurt it. 'Polly!' she hallooed to her sister on the brow – 'coom quick! here's a wench drawed aht in her pit-claes – eh, Lord,

Mr. Wright, landlord of the Three Crowns, Standish Gate ('a rather tall man') and two broo-wenches from the Mains. bought March 1865.
Carte by Miss Louisa Millard of Wigan. (page 86)

□ *Pit brow girls just before starting their work, 1893.* Albumen (?) print by Thomas Taylor of Platt Bridge, near Wigan. (above)

just look!' and all the other lasses, 5 in number, came running down to see.

Two had been thrutching corves, and 3 filling trucks: they were all stout robust young women of twenty or so, in trousers and thick jackets or coats. One had worked in factory, but liked pit better. They looked with grave wonder at the photograph, till some man from the brow called – 'Polly, wench, bring thy spade!' and then they ran back to work. And my Margaret, who had more life and soul in her than all the rest had, cried out to me 'Goodbye! Aw'm going to warm mysel!' and stamping and folding her arms, darted off at a smart run and disappeared.

. . . I went down, and on the No. 1 pit close by. Here were about 9 young women working as at No. 2, and equally stout and healthy. . . . As I left them, a woman in peacoat and fustian trousers came out of the engine house in a leisurely manner, her hands in her pockets. She had a very striking face: aquiline features, a strong jaw and bold chin, and hazel eyes so large and keen that to meet their gaze was like breasting the blow of a mountain breeze. She said she was 37 years old, but looked nearly ten years younger: she was strong and square-built, but not coarse nor large. And who was this beauty, whose face begrimed as it was, was so handsome and powerful and expressive? Why, she was a mere quadruped. She had been brought up in service, she said: but of her own accord had left that calling, and gone down a coal pit, about 15 years ago, to work as a drawer [that is, seven years after women were prohibited by law from working underground]. Of course she went as a man; dressed in men's clothes and passed as a man; but she liked it, and liked the work. Did she draw with the belt and chain? 'Yes', she said: 'I was harnessed to

the corves, with a belt round my body and the chain between my legs, hooked on to the corves.' And did not the harness hurt you? 'No; my breeches kept the chain from hurting my legs.' And you went on your hands and feet, just as a horse goes on four legs? 'Yes, just the same', she said simply: 'and the roads was rough – there was no rails when I draw'd; it was over my wrists in mud, often'. 'I used to draw the corves 200 or 300 yards' she went on; 'I could do it easily; I don't mind going on my hands and feet for that distance, and more; oh no! And it did not make my hands very hard, using them as if they was feet; nor harder than they are now.' All this the handsome brighteyed woman told with quiet unaffected candour. 'I liked it!' she said with emphasis: 'but when I'd been working down a month, they found out I was a woman, and I was turned out: and since then I've worked on pit-brow and worn breeches, as I'm doing now.'

I was just going to ask the name of this mulier formosa,* when I was interrupted. On the brow I had seen afar off a big rough looking man *in a hat*: unique phenomenon. And now this same man came suddenly up unawares, placed himself before me, and said with loud voice and angry tone to me 'What may your business here be? Go off!' I stared, and declined to tell my business without knowing who my questioner was. 'What's that to you?' he cried: 'you're not welcome here: go off!' But as I did not go, he, after more reproaches, added, hoarsely 'You want to know my authority; well, I'm the proprietor of this colliery; and I don't want *you* here; and I tell you to *go off!*' and he clenched his fist. I then apologized for having intruded, adding that if I had been properly addressed I should have done so at first. To which 'Sammy†

*'beautiful woman'

†Samuel Stock was the owner of extensive collieries at Blackleyhurst and was also active in local banking affairs. Munby seems to have been oblivious to any disruption of work he was causing at the pit brows he visited. Sammy Stock may have been particularly sensitive about this woman having worked underground, as he had in the past been taken to court for breaking the law by employing women below ground after it had been made illegal to do so.

Pit brow girls, 1867–78
Cartes by John Cooper of Wigan.

Stock' (for it was he) replied, 'I don't want your apologies: go off!' and turning to the woman, who had stood by silent, he added roughly 'Go to your work!'

She went, meekly enough: and I also took my way. It was worth remarking that this the only act of rudeness that was ever offered to me at a coal pit, came from the master, and not from the workpeople, male or female.

Monday 10 September 1866. It was noon now, and they were just knocking off work on the brow [at Bottom Place Pit, Ince], for dinner; girls catching up their jackets to run home, or getting out their dinner cans in the cabin, where I found half a dozen lasses seated, holding in their black hands meat pasties or hunches of bread, and making short work of them: Ann Prescot was there, with her broad shoulders, and a wonderful red and yellow kerchief round her head, setting off the grimy darkness of her handsome face. She had promised to go and be 'draw'd aht' at Cooper's; but now she said she dared not, her father had forbidden it. Sarah Fairhurst also, whom I found in the cabin at the sister-pit close by, along with Maggie Taberner and a man, was as unwilling as ever to be photo'd; which is a pity, as she is one of the nicest and most robust of her class.

She stood up erect against the cabin door, whilst I measured her height; and she is 5 feet *nine.*

The men – for another came in – urged her to go to Cooper's; and I stood facing her, holding her hand in mine, trying to persuade her: but her ignorance and her modesty deserved respect, and I ceased to press it.

Tuesday 11. I went to Cooper's, and bought some photos; among them, happily, the belles of Bottom Place Pit, Sarah and Ellen Fairhurst, in their Sunday clothes.

Wednesday 10 September 1873. I reached Wigan, . . . and walked up Scholes, the main street of the colliers' quarter of Wigan, to call on Ellen Grounds, the nearest of my friends, and learn from her the news of the pits. . . . Close by St. Catherine's church, on Mount Pleasant, a vast open space which lies waste because of the pits beneath it, in Scholefield Lane, a row of little redbrick dwellings. In the window of No. 108, the passing child observes inviting comfits, brandyballs, and penny whistles. Here I knocked; and opening the door, whom should I see but Miss Ellen Grounds, wiping of the deal table in the middle of the brick floor. Miss Ellen, who is now four and twenty, was in woman's clothes, this time; a decent brown stuff frock with sleeves, and a white apron; and her light brown hair was knotted up simply behind, and brushed smooth against her comely cheerful face. She looked up, with a puzzled smile. 'What, Ellen, dun yo know ma'?' 'yea, Ah do – why, yo was here better than three year sin'!' she answered; and gave me her hand, which was clean, and in spite of her manly work was neither coarse nor very hard. A fire was blazing in the grate, of course; on one side of it sat Ellen's father the brooman, who was fresh from work and was black; on the other, her handsome old mother, in a blue striped kirtle and a close frilled cap. And by the window, with his feet on the settle, sat her young brother, a collier; who never spoke a word the whole time I was there, except Yes or No – in answer to me. 'Sit yo doon!' said the damsel, handing me a woodenseated chair; and the old couple added 'Aye, sit yo doon!' But why did Ellen wear this effeminate dress? Why was she so exasperatingly clean, and the coaldust gone from her hands? Because she has been 'playing' all the week, stopping away from the pit, to attend to her mother, who is unwell. Ellen has left Rose Bridge pits; she now works at Pearson & Knowles's Arley Mine pit, a mile off across the canal. . . . Mrs Grounds had already said that many a mon likes to wed a pit-wench, because she can keep him, or nearly so. And has Ellen got a sweetheart? 'Naa, Ah lost him', said Ellen, calmly enough. 'He died

Ellen Grounds, filler, of Rose Bridge Pits, aged 17. 1866.
Carte by Robert Little of Wigan.

Ellen Grounds, collier, in Sunday dress, 1866.
Carte by Robert Little of Wigan.

Ellen Fairhurst, Bottomplace Pit. Height 5 feet 9 in.
Carte by John Cooper of Wigan, probably taken in 1866.

o' smallpox'. said her father; 'but he's left her summut to remember him by.' What, that two year old child on the floor? 'Yah!' said Ellen, taking up the lad and fondling him, which indeed she had done before: and added, in reply to what I said, But Ah never had a chance te marry him, yo know!' Neither she nor her parents were ashamed of the matter, though they are all decent folk. Her father was evidently fond and proud of the child. Ellen, who has been a factorygirl and a maid of all work, and has now worked 9 years at broo, said she means to work at pit 'as long as the Lord'll gie me strength,' and added 'an t'lad'll work an' all.'

Then we talked about being 'drawed aht.' Ellen said she had been 'drawed aht' twice 'i' my pit claes', and has seen her own picture hanging up for sale. It is not good however; and I asked if she could not come tomorrow, as she is 'playing'. Her father and mother both concurred; and Ellen never thought of objecting to walk through the town in her pit

dress; which indeed dozens of pit girls do daily, and go of their own accord to be drawed aht in that attire, in order that they may send the picture to absent friends. So Ellen promised to come tomorrow in her pit clothes to Wigan marketplace and Clarence Yard. The only question was, whether she should come with a black face or a clean one. She observed that one often looks just as well with a black face; and I left the point to her discretion; but asked to see her working dress. 'Here's t' bonnet,' she said bringing out of the scullery a pitgirl's wadded hood bonnet, sound and fairly clean; 'and here's mah bedgoon'; which was of pink cotton, patched with bits of blue. And the breeches? 'Naa' said Ellen, with creditable shamefastness, 'mah breeches is oopstairs, Ah cannot fotch 'em dahn!' Her father and mother, however, both counselled her to bring them; and I was glad of the opportunity of examining this unique garment. So Ellen went upstairs, and came down again with her trousers over her arm.

Shevington, 1863.
Detail from an albumen print by an unidentified photographer. Note the primitive nature of the pit head, and the basket-type corves used to bring the coal up from underground.
(page 90, above)

Wenches at Rose Bridge Pits (Case & Morris's) Wigan. 1865. Note the comparative height of the girls and the man.
Half of stereo pair by S. S. Lees of St. Helens. (page 90, below)

Taken at Shevington, 1864.
Carte by T. G. Dugdale of Wigan.

Pit brow girl. *Shevington, 1867.*
Carte by T. G. Dugdale of Wigan.

'Them's mah breeches,' she said; 'they're patched that Ah connot tell t'maan piece on 'em; they was a pair o'men's owd breeches when Ah gat 'em, and Ah've wore em t'nahn year at Ah've worked at pits!' And they were still good; a pair of trousers made up of patches of cloth and cotton and linen of various colours, but toned down by coaldust to a blackish brown. They were warmly lined and wadded, especially at the knees, to protect them when kneeling among coals or crawling up the shoot; a garment well fitted to keep warm the legs of a woman doing outdoor work. And (which spoke well for the fair wearer) the *inside* of the trousers was clean. They had button holes round the top. How do you keep them on? I asked. 'Well' said Ellen, in mere simplicity and not in coarseness, 'there's a many wenches ties string round their waasts; but Ah've getten a good backsahd, at keeps me breeches oop!' She who made this dreadful speech is a fair and comely English girl; homekeeping, industrious, and virtuous according to her lights.

Thursday 11. Showery a.m.; fine day, breezy and sunny.

At 5.30 a.m. I was awoke by the tramp of the factory girls. My window at the Royal Hotel looks upon the market place: I got up, and saw the broad street busy with women and girls, all in clogshoon and most of them with shawls over their heads, all tramping to work in groups of two and three, and talking broad Lancashire audibly. Hundreds of them; and hardly any men. The sun had not risen; it was dawn, and great rosy clouds were in the west. I went to bed again; and thought that after all, my Hannah's life has been a harder and rougher, and a far more humbling, life than that of these girls – or even that of the pit wenches. And yet, what a difference in the result! About ten, I went through the market place, and down Clarence Yard to the humble abode of Mrs. Little, photographer, and cab-owner's wife. I enquired for Ellen Grounds. 'Hes yon wench coom?' 'Yea, hoo hes,' said

Mrs. Little; and she and her grown up daughter wore a puzzled smile, as if they were about to show me some strange creature. A moment afterwards, Ellen herself came out of the kitchen; and she was in her pit clothes, as she had promised. 'Well, Ellen, yo've coom!' 'Yah, Ah's coom, Sir!' said the collier-lass, who looked vastly better, and also bigger, in her working dress, than she did last night in woman's clothes. She wore her wadded bonnet, the front part tied tight over the forehead, and the hood encircling her head like an aureole; her loose bluepatched cotton bedgown made her full bust and broad shoulders look larger still; below it, came her striped skirt, gathered up round the hips; and under that her breeches – the pair she showed me last night – and her iron clogshoon. She had forgotten to bring her topcoat; and first she tried on a coat belonging to Mrs. Little's son, a big lad; but it was too small for her; so she tried a rough coat, like her own, of *Mr.* Little's; and it fitted her well. Then she was furnished with a spade, to represent her great pit shovel. She shouldered the spade in workmanlike fashion, buttoned her coat, and stood readily and well, as I posed her; and she was taken, first in that guise, and then without the coat; I standing beside her, to show how nearly she approached me in size.

Monday 14 September 1874. I walked on across the canal to Middle place Pit . . . I went up on the brow, and found that the thrutchers were all men; where the women were, I could not see, till Alice Haydock's black but comely young face appeared, looking up at me from below the flooring, through a small trap door which had a rough ladder under it, leading down into darkness. When I had squeezed myself down the ladder, I found Alice and her two mates immured in a small black hold, floored with rough coal, on which the lasses had flung their rough top coats; for here they mostly work all day, only swinging themselves down into the barges or the railway trucks, when they are ordered to

Female collier from Rose Bridge Pits, height about 5 feet 9. taken 10 August 1869. Carte by Robert Little of Wigan.

Pit girl with oil lamp, *1869.*
Carte by Miss Louisa Millard of Wigan.

Pit brow girl, *1867.*
Carte by Robert Little of Wigan.

Miner and pit brow woman, *1869.*
Carte by Miss Louisa Millard of Wigan.

Pit brow girls, *1868.*
Carte by G. I. Moore of Liverpool.

Pit brow girls, *1874.*
Carte by Robert Little of Wigan.

a b c d
e f g
h i j

load. The steep coal shoot passes through their cave, and every few minutes a load of some ten cwt. of coal is discharged from above, and fills the hold with suffocating black dust, which escapes into the air after settling freely on the faces and arms and clothes of the women. They care not for it, but with their great rakes they guide and sort the fallen coal, till Alice bends to her great iron rod and sets the load free again, to fall upon another set of girls in the barges or the trucks below. *Alice Haydock* is a fine brawny lass of twenty, with a healthy blooming face and a quiet manner; but her voice (with much shouting, perhaps) was rough and hard, like her big hands. She has worked six years at the pits. One of her mates was *Margaret Pallett*, a stout hearty woman of 45, with a very black face. She worked belowground in the pit, thrutching corves, from ten years old to 18, when the women were turned out. When I said, Did you like it? She gave me the usual answer: 'Like it? Aye! an Oi'd gaw dahn again, if tha'd let ma'!' We had not talked five minutes, when down came the roaring cloud of coal dust: speech became impossible; the third woman, across the shoot, was lost to view; and we three were blackened once more. And just then came another noise overhead, sudden and tremendous. The women, always working in this blind hole, among flying coal and whirling blackness* and thumping shattering sounds, did not mind it much. Margaret started a little; but Alice did not wince, and only said calmly, 'It'll be t'cheean's brokken'. And so it was; one of the great bearing chains of the pit's headgear. Men crowded the flooring above, to set it right; and the three women were ordered up by the gaffer to another job; filling railway trucks at the other side of the brow. They left their great iron rakes, and climbed the ladder and through the trap door, in their trousers, as easily as sailors, and went to get their spades.

Wednesday 18 September 1878. Then down into the village of Ince; and found the Fairhursts' dwelling, in a row, and went in, to see poor *Ellen Fairhurst*. She, the pride of Ince, the bonniest cleanest collierlass, whose sunny face and robust frame and massive brown arms made up the ideal of a bright hardworking country wench, was now lying in the back kitchen, on an antique settle of black oak, heaped with bed clothes, and her blue topcoat above her, dying of a consumption. She smiled, and gave me her hand – hard still, but now white and thin, like her arm. But the sunny hue of her face was there still, and her cheeks were flushed, and her large eyes and regular white teeth more notable than ever. Her dark hair lay loose on the pillow; she looked quiet and sweet as a lady, while she talked to me, low and gasping, in her broad honest Lancashire. 'Aye, it's ight moonths sin' Ah left pit,' she said: 'doctor says Ah'm worse, an' parson, yea, wa've nobbut te tell him, an' he'll coom.' 'Hoo's very waak,' said her pleasant married sister . . .

Poor Ellen! It is not pitwork that has killed her; for washing slack was her work, and she wrought under cover, in her high airy cabin where I have so often seen her. She looked at me for the last time, and said 'Thank ye, Sir,' as I wrung her hand at parting; and her rough old mother, sitting by in the chimney corner, sobbed and cried as I shook hands with her.†

a) Pit brow girl, *1869*.
Carte by Miss Louisa Millard of Wigan.

b) *Wigan collier girl given to me by W. Whitley, 1865.*
Carte by an unidentified photographer.

c) Pit brow girl, *1865*.
Carte by John Cooper of Wigan.

d) Pit brow girl, *1870*.
Carte by Robert Little of Wigan.

e) Pit brow girls, *1868*.
Carte by G. I. Moore of Liverpool.

f) Pit brow girl. *Top Place Pit, taken 1873*.
Carte by Robert Little of Wigan.

g) Unidentified pit brow woman. *Ince Hall pits – 1863*.
Carte by John Cooper of Wigan.

h) Pit brow girl, *1867*.
Carte by Robert Little of Wigan.

i) Pit brow girl, *1866*.
Carte by Robert Little of Wigan.

j) Pit brow girls, *1870*.
Carte by John Cooper of Wigan.

*The coal dust must have troubled many of the pit brow girls. Munby saw one girl 'who had weak eyes, and wore large blue spectacles, to protect them from the coal dust'. On other occasions he saw one girl wearing 'a piece of crape' across her face to keep out the dust, and another among women working amidst clouds of dust where he could glimpse 'the gleam of a brass earring on a black neck', who 'wore leather blinkers, like a vicious horse, over her eyes, to keep off the showers of coal.' Because of the coal dust blowing about, Munby noted that 'a moist drizzling day' was the best for seeing coalpits.
†Ellen Fairhurst died later that year.

2: South Wales Mine Tip Girls

Sunday 10 October 1869. Got to Swansea by 12.30. I walked down the High Street, to find Andrews the photographer, and found his house, with no one in it but his servant, a strong Welsh lass from H'arfordwest, with a kindly face and large broad hands. She showed me the stock of photographs, but we found no minetip girls among them. She had seen these girls; has a brother a pitman; but thinks they 'work like slaves', and that 'Government ought to stop em'. How would you like it, said I, if Government was to stop your being a servant? 'Well Sir' said she naïvely 'I should be glad! I wouldn't be a servant, not if I'd the means to live without it.'

There was, however, a photographer in South Wales who took a particular interest in women working on the mine tips, and unfortunately Munby did not know of him. W. Clayton, a photographer of Iron Street, Tredegar, took a large number of *carte* portraits – both outdoors and in the studio – of mine-tip girls in the 1860s. An album of these *cartes* has survived and is now in the collection of the Gallery of English Costume, at Manchester, inscribed 'C. B. Crisp 29th. April 1865', and all the photographs reproduced here are taken from it.* Nothing is known of C. B. Crisp, but one can gain some insight into his (or possibly her) motives for collecting these photographs from a newspaper cutting which is pasted at the front of the album:

□ Tip girls, Tredegar, *c.* 1865.
Cartes by W. Clayton of Tredegar.
(above and pages 97 and 98)

Travellers see strange sights, and strangers coming into the iron districts of South Wales often make strange remarks. It is however, a fine sight at night to see the blaze issuing from the numberless fires of the Tredegar Iron Works, illuminating the sky far over the distant hills. These immense works occupy a large area of ground and employ several thousand hands and continually send forth flames from furnaces burning some hundred tons of coal. Surrounding the town and the works are what strangers call the 'Black Mountains', which are the refuse and burnt coal tipped and heaped together from the works, and, being accumulated, forms in the course of time a range of semi-mountains, until these tips consolidate and get covered with verdure; and on part of some of the old tips, George-town, Vale-terrace, and rows of houses have lately been built. On the top of these tips, rails are laid down for trams, to carry away the useless mass of cinder from the fires and furnaces, and on arriving at the extremity, the trams are tipped and by this means the black mountains or tips are everlastingly on the increase in length and height. To do this work women and girls are employed and wear a peculiar style of dress, consisting of a short frock and apron, tight to the neck, made of a material resembling hop cloth or fine sacking, red worsted stockings, and lace-up boots heavy with hobnails, tips and toecaps that would pull the legs off some of the ploughmen of the Midland Counties. The bonnet or hat, for it is difficult to discern to which of the classes this head-dress be-

*This album also contains a *carte* of 'Lancashire Coal Women' – pit brow girls in fact – by John Cooper of Standishgate, Wigan. It seems that Mr. Clayton's *cartes* of mine tip girls, like those of the Wigan girls, were on sale as curiosities. A duplicate of one of the *cartes* by W. Clayton in C. B. Crisp's album is in the collection of the National Museum of Wales.

longs, is bedecked with beads, brooches, and feathers, the latter addition in a small way imitating the Prince of Wales plume. In this dress, with faces black with dust and smoke, it is difficult, when elevated fifty or a hundred yards, to discern the sex to which these objects belong; and a gentleman, who evidently had never witnessed such a sight before, on visiting the town of Tredegar recently, expressed his astonishment at making mountains on mountains and inquired what animals those were he saw moving about on the top? In the tempest and the storm, in rain and in snow, in the sun and heat, exposed to all weathers, women and young girls are employed on the tips in South Wales.

from the *Bristol Mercury*, 29 April 1865

Although Munby failed to find portraits of mine tip girls on sale, he was familiar both with their work and that of other labouring women in South Wales, for example at Blaenavon, a few miles from Tredegar:

Friday 22 September 1865. The whole of the upper end of the Blaenavon valley is filled with the coal pits, cokeovens, iron blast-furnaces, and brickworks, of the Blaenavon company. . . . First I came to the brickworks: . . . At the kilns were 10 girls, 3 to each kiln, and a 'shoveller'. They did the whole of the work, with a Gaffer over them. They were all wellgrown healthy lasses, aged from 15 to 21: all wore coarse ragged smocks – 'pinnies' they call them – belted at the waist, and strong laced boots, and kerchiefs tied round head and neck. Some had on hoodbonnets, some wideawakes or mushroom strawhats, with a ribbon or a bunch of hawthorn berries stuck therein. The smocks reach to just below the knee; and under them some of the girls wore short cotton trousers, and some woollen stockings only. . . .

Next came the *cokeovens*, which were on the vast shale-mountains above. I found a great many girls here, some digging and sifting coke; some emptying coke-trams by the shovelfuls into the ovens . . . some standing in the railway trucks and unloading them of the ironstone. . . . Thence to the *blastfurnaces* near, where the overlooker, a Welshman named Powell . . . showed me round, strangers being not allowed to go alone. Numbers of grownup young women were working here, but no mere girls, the work being too hard. Some were filling and wheeling barrows of ironstone; but most were engaged, inside certain wooden sheds, in *breaking stones*: breaking the big lumps of ironstone, ready for fusing. A man first reduces these to about $\frac{1}{2}$ or $\frac{1}{4}$ of a cwt., and then the girls smash them up. They use heavy hammers, larger than those of roadside workers, and stand at the heaps and pound away with a will, lifting the hammer over their heads and bringing it down with manly skill and force. Fine strong girls they were; barearmed and sinewy, with kerchiefs only on their heads: and yet not more robust than the best of the others I had seen. They break stones thus from 6 a.m. to 6 p.m. every day, only ceasing for breakfast and dinner; and earn 6/ to 7/ a week. 6 to 6 are the hours everywhere about here. Most of the stonebreakers were of a yellowishgrey colour, like the stone: but one lass with stout bare arms, who was breaking Northumbrian ore, was red like a red Indian; her face, which was comely, and her limbs, all glowing with ruddy sweat. Some of these girls too had trousers on under their short smocks. I saw so many girls at these Blaenavon works that it was impossible to count them: Mr. Powell could not or would not say how many, but there must have been 100 to 200. And all were young, and all or nearly all unmarried, and all healthy and robust and civil. 'They run much of a size', as Mr. P. said, to wit about 5 feet 2 or 4: 'and we boast', said he, 'that they are the finest women of the kind anywhere'. . . . 'If it wasn't for the girls here', he added as we stood looking at the female stonebreakers, 'I dont know what the ironworks would do'.

3: Women Miners in Belgium

Monday September 1 1862 [at Charleroi]. I got up early, had coffee in my room, and set out before 8 to walk to the coalmines of Mambourg.

Passed through the market and streets of Charleroy . . . and up the long street of the haute ville to the fortifications. . . . A little above the last drawbridge you reach the brow of the hill, from which is a view of a valley to the left and another hill beyond; a mining country the whole of it. Close by is the first of the pits, 5 in number, belonging to the Societé Anonyme de Charbonnages réunies de Mambourg.

I went to the brow, and learnt from the clerk of the works that no women were employed there. 'But,' he said, 'there are plenty of them below.' This was new to me; for at Liège I was told that they have there female colliers aboveground, but none in the mines. 'What!' I said 'do you mean to say there are women down here – working underneath the ground where we stand?' He replied 'Yes: we have only a few here – ten or so – this is a small pit: but at the large ones there are hundreds.' I at once resolved to go down and see them: here was a novel aspect of female labour, and one there is no longer a chance of seeing in England.* . . . The pit brow looked exactly like those in England: two clerks in blouses, very civil young fellows, helped me to a set of pit clothes, which I put on, leaving my own in their charge: to wit, blouse and trousers to match, with coarse shirt, and stout miner's leather hat. Arrayed in these, I spent nearly two hours with the clerks, for the overlooker who should conduct me was busy below. I learnt from them, and found for myself afterwards, that the mining

employments of the two sexes are just the converse of those in England. Here about Charleroy men only (tireurs) are wrought at the brow, pushing the corves; whilst down in the pits, the number of women labourers exceeds that of the men. In this pit for instance, they have 600 colliers, of whom about 350 are young women and girls.

About one the overlooker came up; the fair lampiste brought me a Davy; and I entered the cage with my ferocious looking guide; the three chargeurs looking on and grinning. They were not uncleanly wenches, considering: drest in short coarse skirts, jackets, and a kerchief to hide the hair, and sabots. One of them had immense broad masculine hands, bigger than the men's. We went down the shaft in about two minutes; crouching down in the cage, in smoke and darkness, with water dropping on us from above. 'Enough to appal the stoutest heart' one might say: yet this is the way in which some three hundred – nay thousands of – girls and young women descend daily to their labour; six in a cage, which seemed to me scarce big enough for us two.

We touched the bottom – or seemed to do so – with a jerk, and crept out into the midst of a group of male colliers.

Thence, with another guide, an old miner, along the main way, some six feet high; meeting trains of large waggons, drawn by horses and these led by boys. After walking a good way we turned into a narrower lower passage, about five feet high; lined with rough stone and propped with posts, and very dimly lit at intervals by fixed lamps. We had gone fully a quarter of a mile from the shaft, when I began to hear female voices mixed with the rumble of approaching wheels. It

*Louis Simonin reported in 1867 that women no longer worked in French mines, and that although women worked in Belgian pits 'such cases become every day more and more rare.'[1] In Germany it was not made illegal for women to work underground until 1891.[2]

PEFFERLAW PUBLIC LIBRARY

was strange to hear them in those black and miry hollows: presently the waggons met us – large corves, but not so big as the horse wains. They were being pushed along by several hurriers. I lifted my lamp as the first passed me – it was a boy: the second was in male clothes too, but she was a girl, so I stopped and examined her. A nicelooking maiden she was of sixteen or so; drest, as they all are, in a greyish white sacking shirt with sleeves, breeches of the same material, woollen stockings and strong nailed boots, and a coarse white kerchief tight round her head. We went on, and presently came to a group of girls, all drest in breeches and shirts etc like the first. . . . They were of different ages; some children of 12 or 14, some stout girls of 18; some grown young women, broad-shouldered and strong, and in their male dress looking nobly robust. Two things struck me at once; the comparative cleanliness of these girls and their white clothing (at least in the dim light); I saw only one or two whose faces were really blackened, and the hands alone were black in all: and their good looks. Most of them were extremely pretty, and feminine too; scarcely one who looked like a man, even in trousers.

We passed through a grim door into a gallery only four feet high, along which we worked our way for some two hundred yards to the end, where was a getting place: a large sloping cave, where men were lying on their sides hewing coal. This work is done by men only; though my guide said he had known a strong young woman who worked as a getter and did it as well as a man.

When we had seen this I found that some corves had arrived empty, with a couple of girls; and for the first time I noticed that one of these girls had harness on over her clothes. A leather thong was fastened round each shoulder, and the two met behind in a broad thick strap, as stout and large as the traces of a carthorse. This hung down the girl's back as she stood up, and to the lower end of it a strong rope was attached, with a chain and

iron hook at bottom, which dangled on the ground at her heels. The maiden was a hurrier, and her business was to draw the waggons, while a comrade pushes behind. She was a bonny lass and a stout, and she said she would draw me back in one of the empty corves: so I clambered in and crouched down, the roof being so low, while she fastened the hook of her harness to a large ring in front of the corve. I gave the signal, and she set off at a slow trot, bending nearly double as she ran and only not going on all fours, and bore me and the waggon along, a second girl pushing at the other end. It was a strange experience: by the light of my Davy I could see before me the harness and the hind legs as it were of my human steed; all else was dark: only, I was at the bottom of a coal pit, in a waggon which was drawn by a woman in man's clothes, who wore the gear and fulfilled the function of a beast of draught. That however is sentiment: the fact was that the two girls tooled merrily along, shouting to others ahead to get on, and finally brought me through the door and *under* the windlass to the crossways. As I got out, it was obvious to pat my steed on the shoulder and say 'Mais vous êtes un bon cheval!' and she laughed and looked pleased at the compliment. . . .

I came up the shaft, changed and washed, thanked my friends, and left with my original guide. . . .

It was now near three, and I returned quickly into Charleroy as I came; calling at a photographer's, where I was agreably surprised to find a whole series of portraits of collier girls, taken *in the mines* by electric light. They were done at Gilly, a place which is 'all mines' and lies about a quarter of an hour beyond Mambourg. . . .

At 7.10 I left Charleroy [by train], passing numbers of ironworks and pitmouths near, but it was too dusk to see them, and reached Namur by 8.30. Walked up to the Hotel de Belle Vue, and in my room there have been writing this, listening to the chimes and the silence.

A few weeks previously Munby had visited the International Exhibition of 1862 in London. There he would almost certainly have seen French photographs taken by electric light. Nadar's photographs taken in the catacombs and sewers beneath Paris excited considerable interest as the first photographs taken underground. They were taken – probably in 1861 – by electric light powered by Bunsen batteries, but the exposure time required was eighteen minutes, and when Nadar wished to depict figures, he had to use life-size dummies. And if one looks closely at the photographs bought by Munby at Charleroi it becomes clear that they are taken not underground by electric light, but on the surface by daylight in a specially constructed mock-up of an underground gallery. In one you can see that a false roof has been constructed over the 'underground passageway', and in another you can see that the rails laid down end abruptly to the right below the crouching miners.

This series of photographs was taken, probably in 1861, by Prosper Bevièrre of Charleroi, and was exhibited by him with the title *Ouvriers houilleurs au travail*.

a) Two Belgian pit girls. *Gilly 1862.*

b) Belgian pit girl and miner. *Gilly 1862.*

c) Belgian pit girls hauling coal wagon. *Gilly 1862.*

d) Belgian miners and pit girls. *Gilly 1862.*

Pit girls who worked underground. *Gilly, près de Charleroy, 1863.*
Outdoor cabinet portrait by Prosper Bevièrre of Charleroi.

The 1860s saw various attempts to take underground photographs by burning magnesium wire and ribbon – magnesium became available commercially in 1864 – but of course the risk of triggering off catastrophic explosions below ground by using the early forms of 'flashlight' in coal mines which contained combustible gases ruled out such experiments in 'fiery mines'.* Munby bought a cabinet portrait of five pit girls from Prosper Bevièrre of Charleroi and it seems that the large photographs of male and female miners are by him – Munby only marked them *Gilly 1862*. In the Exposition des Arts Industriels at Brussels in 1861 Prosper Bevièrre had exhibited and received a *mention honorable* for photographs entitled *Ouvriers houilleurs au travail*,[3] and I believe that it was copies of these that Munby bought in 1862.

Both Munby and Émile Zola found the image of young women miners wearing men's clothes particularly interesting. In *Germinal* (published in 1885) Zola described Catherine Maheu getting ready for work: 'She stepped into her miner's trousers, put on her coarse linen jacket and fastened her blue cap over her knot of hair. In these clean, Monday-morning clothes she looked like a little man, and the only trace left of her sex was a slight swing of the hips.' And on another occasion when she had changed out of her working clothes: 'he recognised Catherine . . . At first he could not believe it: could this girl in the dark blue frock and bonnet really be the same young scamp he had seen in trousers with her hair screwed up under a cloth cap?'[4] Munby bought a copy of *Germinal* in August 1886 and an English edition the following December, but his diary does not provide us with his opinion of the book.

Whatever Munby's reaction to Zola's novel was, it was unlikely to have been similar to the view expressed by a commentator in *The Saturday Review* in 1887: 'Nobody disputes that the exclusion of women from underground work many years ago, and the consequent prevention in England of the sordid horrors of *Germinal*, was a very wise thing.'[5] The Belgian pits had offered to Munby not a vision of sordid horror but a chance to see strenuous female labour denied him in British pits by the Act of 1842.

*And as the miners photographed by Bevièrre carry safety lamps, there *was* the danger of explosion in the mine where they worked.

4: Fishergirls of the Yorkshire Coast

Monday 31 October 1864. At 11.30 I went by train to Filey, arriving at 12. . . .

I found a civil photographer (W. Fisher) near the station, and had a talk with him. He often takes photos, he says, of Filey fishgirls, for artists, and sends them to London, even to *Florence*, to an English artist there. The girls will come readily, if you give them a copy of the portrait.

They work harder than the men, ashore. Poor things! But then the men are almost always afloat, you see. They are big strong lasses, with hands and arms 'very large', says Mr. Fisher: they wear a bonnet with a cushion atop for loads to rest on, a cotton frock kilted up over a short red kirtle, black or grey woollen stockings, and strong shoes. In the late autumn and early spring they go in troops to Scarborough to gather flithers* for bait: travelling thither by rail . . . Then they walk on, beyond Scalby mostly, fill their creels or sacks, and *walk back loaded* all the way to Filey.

Tuesday 14 February 1865. Beautiful day. Sun, blue dappled sky, cold air. . . . Walked with Miss E. Wood, 11–1.30, to Brig.† The tide was lowest about 12.30, and going and coming we saw 13 women on the scars on the Filey side of the Brig, and about as many men. . . . A striking contrast, between these great stalwart lasses, striding freely over the scars,‡ and my small slim companion, who trod them hardly with the aid of my hand: her small gloved hand too, and those large red bare ones – one smacked her arms across her chest to and fro for warmth with a vigour that astounded Miss E. W.. They told us that the Filey women start today for the first time for Cloughton, [a few miles north of Scarborough] flithering. About 20 go today by the 9 a.m. or 3pm train, with fisher-women's tickets, 3d. each 3rd. class, and will return on Friday by train reaching Filey at 5 p.m., after walking to Scarbro. These tickets began about 6 years ago, by the help of some ladies. Before that, the women used to walk to Cloughton *and also to Robin Hood's Bay* for bait, and back the same day – 44 miles! (so they protested) starting at 12.30 or 1 a.m.. Now they only walk from Cloughton to Robin Hood's Bay in one day and back. *'T'women-tickets'*§ said one 'is 3d..'

Tuesday 21. Grey fair day: no wind nor snow, and a very slight thaw, but the snow of yesterday thick on the ground: and oh the sweet silence that deep snow brings! all things muffled and still; no sound of wheels or footsteps but sledgebells lightly ringing. I went, with Louisa, to Inskip's, and then to King's and got my photos of Lizzie Williamson, Margaret Eaves, and Annie Born. At 3.15 p.m. I met the Filey train. 13 fishwomen came by it, my friends of Friday and others – but Annie B., her sister, and Sally Cammish, had come at 9 a.m. and gone on. All their baskets they flung in a heap on

W. FISHER   FILEY

Annie Born and Hannah Hunter, 1867.
taken in my presence.
Carte by Walter Fisher of Filey.

*Limpets, which have shells shaped like a flat cone, and adhere firmly to the rocks on the seashore. They had to be prised off with a 'flitherknife'.
†Filey Brig is a long rocky promontory at the northern end of Filey Bay.
‡Scars are sloping shelves of rock – a grey shale in this area – which are exposed as the tide goes out.
§They were marked FISHWOMAN

the platform and crowded round me to look at Annie's picture – it was 'life's self', 'her very effidge!' They were some minutes packing the baskets on each others' backs, and then they filed out of the station and down the town, a long line of stout picturesque women and lasses, well knit and girt and laden. Each had 7 or 8 'tides', i.e. baskets weighing 1 stone or more when full, fastened with ends on her back and shoulders, and all resting on a pad on the hips. The baskets all empty except 1 or 2 which held food, and knitting. Folks stopped to look at 'em; boys shouted 'flitherlasses!' . . . I walked with them to Burniston, talking all the way.

Thursday 9 March. [at Cloughton] Awoke in dark and heard voices in the village street. Looked out at 3.40 a.m. and dimly saw 5 Filey women struggling up the hill past my window, against a storm of sleet.* They were Jane Haxby and others, starting for Robin Hood's Bay. 2 more followed. 5 more passed at 5 a.m. – Jane Capleby jun. and others – 14 passed at 6 a.m. and 4 at 6.15, all striving against wind and snow, which had made the face of the country white. Annie and Sarah were with those at 6 – all the parties were talking loud and cheerful, and laughing. The first party had 9 miles of moor to walk in the storm – they were talking of spots to 'get good shelter'. At 6 it was dawn, and some looked up for me and cried 'he's oop it winder!' All Cloughton was still asleep.

The gathering of bait was crucial to the Yorkshire fishing industry and was left almost entirely in the hands of the women and girls of the fishing communities from Staithes in the north to Flamborough in the south. The bait required varied according to the time of year as the seasons dictated a natural cycle of change in the fishermen's catch.

The season for 'long-lining' – winter and early spring – coincided with some of the most bitter weather of the year, and the women had to keep working from February until June through rain, snow and gales. Limpets had partly replaced mussels as bait, because mussels were in short supply† Munby reported that: 'Mussels are brought from Boston Deeps [in The Wash] and laid on the Filey side of the brig; and all winter the women fetch them thence at lowtide, whenever the men go out coble fishing.'‡[1] Buoys were positioned as markers to show where the mussels were laid down. Sometimes the women went out as early as 3 o'clock in the morning carrying lanterns in order to gather bait, and it was vital to 'knaw wer awn scars'. When women had to compete for the natural resources of bait available on the seashore, trouble could arise. Munby talked to some women from the important fishing village of Staithes: 'They said about 130 women go for bait

*The previous day he had seen the women sheltering in a gale and snowstorm on the sea shore. As he explained: 'They could get no flithers hardly for the wind was so strong that the tide would not go down.'

†Munby noted in 1878 that liver and herrings were now the winter bait, rather than flithers. Mussels were imported from the Tees and, when these sources could not keep pace with the demands of the fishermen, from as far away as Hamburg.

‡Cobles are the flat-bottomed open fishing boats used on the Yorkshire coast. Fishing from open boats in the North Sea was a dangerous occupation. Munby noted that on one day in 1865, two of the three married women he had talked with had lost husbands by drowning at sea.

from Staithes – but probably more, as the population of the place is 1400. They said that some had gone today to Hunt Cliff by Saltburn, 7 or 8 miles. Some go to Kettleness too, but only on Tuesdays and Fridays. Once Runswick women and Staithes women ''scratted'' each other on the scars, and the Justices divided the week between them.'[2]

All this effort was necessary because the bait had to be fresh. Once mussels or limpets had been *scaaned* (removed from their shells) and a long-line baited, they would last only for a couple of days. If the boats did not put to sea, the women had to clean the decaying old bait off the lines (this was called *mucking*) and put fresh bait on the hundreds of hooks.

During 'herringing' – herring fishing – in the summer and early autumn things were a little easier, and the main job of the fisherwomen was to keep the nets in good repair.

The ceaseless demand for bait drove the fishergirls to extreme measures. To the north of Flamborough Head high chalk cliffs prevented the girls from getting down on to the rocky foreshore which was exposed as the tide receded. They could not make their way along under the base of the cliffs, and considerable quantities of bait in the form of limpets and whelks lay inaccessible but tantalisingly close – between one and two hundred feet below as they looked down from the cliff edge. The women had solved the problem by climbing up and down the cliffs by means of ropes secured by stakes at the cliff top. Not surprisingly, Munby found some local girls who were afraid to climb down the ropes. He told the story of Nan Cross – a teenage girl who managed to get down the 200 foot drop at Gull Neuks but lost her nerve at the bottom. She did not dare to make the ascent, but the rope was the only way off the rocks, which were covered by the tide at high water. Another girl told him: 'Ah ed ta gan all twaa te toon te fetch her father.'[3]

Surprisingly, there were almost no fatal slips as the girls went down and up the fixed ropes hand over hand, without the protection of a safety line. If they had lost their grip, they would have fallen all the way to the base of the cliff. 'Accidents?' said one fishergirl, 'Naw, Ah niver hcerd tell o' nean – Aye, there was wown woman, she *wad* gan doon t'rawp be hersen, foore tahm was, and when t'others coomed tha' foond her laad de-ad upon t'rocks – Bud that's long sin' – foore iver *Ah* begun te gan.'[4] A strong Flamborough girl named Molly Nettleton, who was twenty when he first met her in 1865 and stood 5 feet 5 inches – 'very muscular, rosy, rough' – was Munby's favourite among the fishergirls who climbed the ropes, and she had made her first descent at the age of eleven.

Cullercoats lasses, 1875. Bought at C., 1879.
Carte by unidentified photographer.

Tuesday 15 October 1867. Then we talked about ropes; for Molly and her set have lost the old rope they had among them – 'lads has took it for a net-rawpe' – and cant afford another; whereby they cannot at present go down Brail Head, and other folks go, and get flithers which they should share. And so, I offered to buy a new rope, on condition that Molly should keep it as her own: and when we reached the town, Molly went off to ask the

fishermen what its exact length should be, and I went to Champion's shop, and then fetched her, and we returned to the shop together; and Molly chose a stout well-tarred rope, and it was weighed, and came to 8 and threepence, being 14 pounds' weight. Its length was 24 'faddom': i.e. 144 feet: so that is the height, up and down which the lasses climb at Brail Head. Molly joyously took up the tarry coil, and carried it home on her arm, I going with her. She thanked me as if 24 fathoms of ship's rope were the prettiest present a young woman could have.

Wednesday 16. When I got to Brail Head, there was the stake, on its point of rock; and there was my new rope, hanging from it down the steep incline, and disappearing over the edge of the cliff beneath. I looked down; and far below, upon the broad black scars left bare by the tide, I with difficulty made out certain little moving figures; three men or lads, and three women; one of whom, by her superior size and stature, I knew to be Mary [Molly] Nettleton. I had not stood there long, when looking back landward, I caught sight of Sally Mainprize and her brother, coming towards me at full speed across country, over hedge and ditch. They came up panting and laughing; and asked me to go down with them; which I declined, knowing how poor my climbing would look, by the side of Sally's. So I went to a point near, to see them descend; and they sprang down the steep 'trod' to the stake. Here, Sally, who was most pictur-esquely drest, adjusted her short red petti-coat. Gathering the hinder part in between her knees, and pinning it up, and tying strings round each knee, she converted the loose cumbersome skirt into a pair of easy serviceable breeches; her brother standing by, waiting. Then she stood up and shook herself, ready for the plunge: and nothing could be more striking in its way, than those two figures, standing together on that high and giddy crag, and relieved against the blue sea and the sky: he in his tarry trousers and blue jersey; she in her white jersey sleeves, her lilac curtainbonnet, her deeper lilac frock, gathered up round her waist, her scarlet knickerbockers, and her stockings grey. Sally descended first: she disdained any help to begin with, and literally *ran* down the first few yards of the incline, which is more precipitous than a house roof, and full of loose stones. Then without stopping she seized the rope, and gaily danced, as it were, letting it slip through her hands, as far as the foot of the incline, where it meets the summit of the main wall of cliff. Here, at the corner of the jutting crag, is a ledge, on which before now I have seen this very girl sit at ease, and whistle to the waves.* She now left the rope and sat there, waiting for her brother, who came down much more slowly. Then, spitting on her hands (vulgar creature!) and rubbing them together, she firmly grasped the rope, which John held steady for her, and stepped over the edge. Down she went, light and easy as a sailor, for 70 or 80 feet; sticking her toes into any crevice of the chalk wall, swinging by the rope from point to point, or quietly dropping, hand under hand, till she saw herself near the bottom: then, springing backward (for her face was to the rock) with a bound, she lighted firm on her feet, upon the bare stony platform at the base of the cliff. Without a moment's delay, she picked up her basket, which she had thrown down from above, drew her flitherknife, and strode off seaward across the scars, to work. But even Sally's practised foot was not always safe on the slippery weed: looking up, and raising her arm to wave me a salute, she slipped and fell sideways into a pool; but was up again in no time, uninjured. It was now eleven o'clock; and after an ineffectual attempt to follow in Sally's heroic footsteps down that dizzy slope, I sat down on the clifftop.

Thursday 15 October 1868. [at Flamborough] Towards eleven o'clock, two bait girls appeared near the foot of the cliff, striding and stooping among the wet seaweed. Both were breeched up to the knee: and she, the tall one with the long legs, was evidently Molly. At that Height [about 250 feet], one could not hear their voices; but I saw them clamber up to the base of the rock, and there, Molly seized the rope, tried it with her own weight, and began to mount. Hand over hand, sticking her toes into the crevices of the chalk wall, she went up, as easily as one might walk upstairs; and having thus climbed some 50 feet, she turned round, and with her back to the cliff, worked her way along a level ledge that just supported her heels, to an overhanging point. There, stooping forward as cooly as possible, she hauled up her own full basket and her fellow's, which the girl below first tied to the rope-end. When the baskets came up, she just loosened them, and hoisted them up, with one hand, upon a broader ledge above her head: then, grasping the rope again, she climbed up to it, and sat down. It was the same windy corner-ledge on which Sally Mainprize used to sit and shout and whistle to the ships at sea: about halfway up the lower part of the cliff. For the whole ascent is like a house-gable; first the wall, and then the steep sloping roof above it. Meanwhile the other girl began to climb in like manner; and I went round and descended the rough 'trod' that leads from the cliff-top to the small flat summit of that lower spur of rock, from which the rope hangs down. From hence you see down the whole of the slope, but no further. The rope, knotted to the fixed stake at my feet, was trembling with some unseen weight; and very soon the crown of Molly's lilac hood-bonnet appeared above the lower edge of the slope. Thence, holding her

Flamborough, 1867. 1. on left Molly Nettleton. 2. middle, Sarah Ann Mainprize. 3. [unidentified].
Half of stereo pair by Walter Fisher of Filey. The stereo card bears the title 'Flamborough Views. No. 58. Bait Girls at work.'

Molly Nettleton and Sally Mainprize posing for a stereoscopic photograph taken by Walter Fisher of Filey, which was entitled 'Flamborough Views. Bait Girls "Breeched"'. (page 106, above)

Flamborough Girls Molly Nettleton and Sar' Ann c 1860.
Half of stereo pair by Walter Fisher of Filey. The stereo card bears the title 'Flamborough Views. 61. Bait Girls "Breeched"'. (page 106, below)

*Two years previously he had noted that: 'Sally whistles as she sits on a ledge of rock: and all the lasses put their hands to their mouths and shout to a brig passing near. "Wa offen shoots till em" says Molly "aye an' tha' answers an' all: tha knaw it's Flambro' gells shootin'." Filey girls do the same, as Sarah Jane Cammish said at Cloughton.'

Cullercoats lasses, 1875. Bought at C. 1879.
Carte by unidentified photographer.

Fishergirl, *Filey, 1873.*
Carte by Walter Fisher of Filey.

Fishergirl, *1875.*
Carte by Inskip of Scarborough.

basket in one hand and tugging at the rope with the other, she soon climbed up to the stake; grasped it, and then grasped my offered hand, and flung herself down beside me on the little platform of rock, panting for breath, but smiling. Her comrade followed a moment afterwards, and did the same: she proved to be that quiet comely and seeming-respectable girl, Nan Beilby. Molly wore a little shawl round her shoulders and white jersey sleeves; her cotton frock was pinned up behind, her blue fishing-kirtle was gathered up breeches-wise and tied beneath each knee; brown stockings of her own knitting cased her strong but shapely legs; but they, and her thin worn boots,* were soaked with wading in the pools. Nan, who was drest and breeched in like manner, sat down on the rock-path

above; and when the two had recovered breath, we began a talk, waiting for the others who were still below. We compared the Flambro' folks and the Filey: there is no jealousy, though the women of each place fancy themselves the harder workers. . . . Thus we chatted and sat, for nearly half an hour, waiting, and looking over the grey and hoary sea, which was creeping up the scars. Dense mist clouds, borne by the strong south-west wind, had been sweeping over us, and beating on us with small searching rain, for some time: and the lasses, though they went down the Head at daybreak, had not brought their pilot jackets, and were getting wet through above as well as below. So Molly stood up for a moment, and showing her tall figure at the cliff edge, shouted to the far off

*The following Saturday afternoon he 'bought a pair of fisher boots for Molly Nettleton' in Scarborough, and two years later 'bought a pair of milkwomen's boots for my tall Flamborough lass' in London.

Lizzie Holmes, 16, left, a Scarbro' lass, middle, Alice Ann Simpson, 18, right. 1869. Carte by Walter Fisher of Filey.

Elizabeth Jenk (in front), Fanny Scales (behind), 1871. Carte by Walter Fisher of Filey.

Jaanie Crawford: aged 15, 1871. Carte by Walter Fisher of Filey.

folk, 'Noo then, coom on, we're gahin'!' And at last the rope at our feet began to tremble again. Instantly Molly and Nan started up, saying 'Wa mun gan an' help 'em,' these fearless lasses seized the rope, and before I could speak a word, began to run, Molly first, head-foremost down the dizzy slope of rock, until they both disappeared over the edge of the cliff wall below. I, the man of the party, was left in a ridiculous position; a useless spectator of these vigorous athletics. But before long, the climbers re-appeared, Molly as usual first, and carrying somebody's basket on one arm while she held on to the rope with the other. The other women followed, in single file; Nan, Lizzie Vickerman, a lass whom I did not know before, Mrs. Taylor, and old Jane Holdsworth, who truly said she was getting past this work [she was sixty-one years old]. After them came 3 fisher 'lads', young men; and I observed that they clung to

the rope with both hands in climbing, while the girls used only one hand, steadying their baskets with the other. The little platform of rock was not big enough to hold us all, so the men went on up the 'trod', and the women followed, after letting down their skirts and shouldering their baskets, each of which has its load of flithers neatly covered with sea-weed. Last of all, Molly, strongest and most agile climber of the group, stood by the stake, and hauled in the rope of which she was the owner. I offered to carry the coil, and did so, finding it heavy enough, until Molly insisted that Jan Beilby should relieve me. And so we walked men first and women after, according to the old world fashion, along the brink of the cliffs, and across the open fields into the road at South Side, all in the driving rain.

Thursday 30 December 1869. At Scarborough, I intended to spend the hour of

Unidentified fisherwoman scaaning
(preparing bait), 1876.
Mounted albumen print by Inskip of
Scarborough.

Unidentified fisherwomen mending net,
1876.
Mounted albumen print by Inskip of
Scarborough. (page 111)

Unidentified fisherwomen, 1876.
Mounted albumen print by Inskip of
Scarborough.

waiting at the Spa, having a season ticket.
But an unexpected pleasure awaited me. In
the crowd at the station, a strong and bulky
figure, as of a railway porter carrying luggage, came full tilt against me from behind: I
turned round to see the attacking party, and
beheld with surprise and delight a Filey
flitherlass, wrapt in her coarse, fishing
clothes, and heavily laden, who was forcing
her way, head down, by main strength, on to
the platform. It was Mary Cammish; yellow-
haired lassie of twenty, whose keen and
comely face I knew full well of old: and she
was not alone, but was followed close by four
other Filey women and lasses, drest and harnessed like herself. Such a phalanx of female
strength soon dashed aside the stranger
ladies, and even the strong men, of the crowd;

and silently and without any rudeness,
the five fisherwomen won their way to a
clear space near the trains, and drew up there
in a body, followed and surrounded by a
welldrest mob, who looked astounded at the
strange dress and stalwart forms of the bar-
barian fishergirls. But I, knowing well what
this irruption meant, went among them at
once, and was received with many a welcome
in broad Yorkshire; for the fair ones knew
me all. There was the senior of the party, old
Mrs. Proctor, and Mary Simpson her adopted
daughter; and there was Ann Emmanson,
stout young wife, looking out with round
hardy face from a mountain of coarse warm
clothing; and Mary Cammish, the strapping
young leader; and Lizzie Willis, a strong and
rosyfaced girl of the same age. . . . They took
off their kerchiefs from their bonnets; took off
their jackets, and laid them folded on their
maunds; slipped off a wet skirt or so, and in
general, loosened and lightened their clothing, now that they were under cover. Their
train to Filey did not go for an hour. 'Wat are
ye boon' te deah wahl then?' I asked. 'Ah
deant knaw,' each one said; 'wa've nowt te
deah; wa mun joost walk aboot and keep
wersells warm.' 'Will ye hev a coop o' tea?'
said I. 'Ah dawna weer te get it,' was their
simple answer: they had never thought of
such a thing as a refreshment room. But I,
leaving them to their public toilette, went to
the buffet to reconnoitre. The large eating
room there was far too grand for my maidens;
they would have felt awkward, among mir-
rors and mahogany chairs. And even in the
secondclass refreshment room, I thought it
best to state at once that the tea and bread
and butter which I ordered was for a party of
Filey fisherwomen. I went back to my friends:
who were now disrobed: they accepted my
offer with warmth; and I walked up the
platform at the head of a column of stalwart
lasses, each drest in seaman's jersey, and
short skirt, and shoes that rang iron on the
stones. A number of men were seated on
chairs round the fire in the second class room.

Seeing such young ladies enter in a body, they stared; and stared still more when I asked them to resign their seats, explaining that my friends were women, and were wet and cold. They gave way, however, quietly enough; and I placed the girls in a half circle round the blazing fire. Tea was brought in, and placed on the stove: 'Set it theer, hooney, this gentleman is a friend of ooers,' said old Mrs. Proctor to the feeble servantmaid. I distributed the meal, and Mrs. Proctor, who was the only elderly woman of the party, expressed the thanks of all, and solemnly invited me to tea with her in Lawyer Richison Yard. I edged in a chair in the only vacant place, which was between Lizzie Willis and Mary Cammish, who had her legs stretched out to the fender, to warm her steaming boots. Their spirits revived by the hot tea, the women began to tell me of their adventures at Cloughton; of the snow, the tempest, the waters, they had just gone through. . . . My train left before theirs; and from the carriage window I could still see, among the miscellaneous ordinary throng, those fine seafaring women, standing by their maunds; to me far nobler and more interesting than any one there.

Saturday December 30 1893. I found my favourite Annie Born, at No. 3 Chapel Street [Filey], a decent back street of fisherfolk. She opened the door to me, in her Filey bonnet and cotton frock and white apron; handsome as ever, at 53, and looking like my own Hannah on a smaller scale. Her kitchen too was like Hannah's; and in it were her two big fisherlads; while her daughter, just married, at 20, stood at *her* cottage door close by. Annie knew me at once, and smiled and shook hands, saying 'Eh, coom in, Sir! Ah've offens thowt on ye!' She offered me tea, and we talked of Sar'Ann Cammish, and owd Jaan Chapman, and the Cloughton days of 1864. Annie no longer goes baiting, nor herringing, nor down the rope at Cliff Top. Back to Scarbro', after a pleasant visit.

5: London Milkwomen

Saturday 20 July 1861. Going across Grosvenor Square, I saw a tall graceful woman cross the road in front of me, walking between two milk cans. Her simple bonnet was shabbier than of old, and the little shawl, that did not half cover her broad shoulders, was new to me; but the strong boots and short cotton frock were the same, and the firm elastic tread under her load, and the tall muscular figure too, though it was losing its maidenly fulness, and growing somewhat gaunt. It was Kate O'Cagney, the Queen of the London milk women.* And she is so still; though the soft complexion of her handsome face is changed, as I saw her today, into a weatherbeaten brown, and though the full curves of her sumptuous form are sharpening into lines of strength. It would not be so if she had been a lady – a well-preserved beauty of that Mayfair through which she passes daily, a rustic contrast; but we must work, nous autres – and Kitty is seven and twenty now, and for nine long years she has walked her rounds *every* day, carrying through London streets her yoke and pails, and her 48 quarts of milk, in all weathers, rain or fair.† Long before the Crimean war she did so; and she does still. She has been wet through hundreds of times: she never had an umbrella‡ or an illness in her life. Parasols, veils, gloves, crinoline: she has lived so long among the gaudiest developments of such things, and throughout her youth too; yet she knows no more of them than a savage, and no more thinks of any one of them in relation to herself than if she had never seen it. Talk to her of gloves or veils, indeed! I protest my respect for such a woman is immense; she has been tried in that furnace of London, and not found wanting to her rustic homeliness after all.§

Looking down at her large hands, redder now than ever, I saw with surprise no wedding ring there. 'Well, Kate!' I said in passing; and the stately wench turned halfround but did not stop or start. 'Oh, Sir!' she exclaimed, opening wide her mouth and her large grey

*'Queen Kitty' was the title Munby used to describe her in his diary. He gave nicknames to other milkwomen he got to know by sight – 'Rosyface', 'Coolie', and 'Sims' Brown Duchess'.
†Another milkgirl told him that she had worked for three years without a single day off 'from year's end to year's end; you can't get it, only by being favourite, like, and then, it's hard; but I mean to get a holiday next summer!' A friend told Munby that 'the women at her dairyman's go into the country in carts every morning at 4, to milk the cows, before they begin their rounds here: and only earn 1/- a day.' By 1870 the London dairies were beginning to introduce what Munby described as 'newfangled handcarts' which carried a four-foot-high can containing seventy quarts. The girls could carry 'only' forty or fifty quarts on their shoulders, but could manage to push this larger volume along on three-wheeled dairy carts.
‡In 1872 he saw a milkwoman going to work carrying an umbrella – 'that degrading instrument' – and described her as 'effeminate'.
§For Munby the milkgirls stood for a traditional, unspoilt rural life outside the city. He described one milkgirl with 'a young blooming face, suggestive of cowslips and farmyards', and another who to Munby 'seemed – as all her fellows seem – to bear about her a rural atmosphere: to be standing not in Jermyn Street, but against a visionary background of meadows and farmyards'. The symbol was for him more powerful than the reality. He was not concerned with practical problems of the day such as 'milk' which was adulterated to such an extent that it contained up to 80 percent water, or milk delivered by 'rural maidens' which was sold in dirty cans and began an outbreak of typhoid fever in Marylebone.[1]

a

b

c

d

e

f

eyes. 'So you are not married, after all?' 'No Sir' she answered, with a sly shamefaced smile and a downcast look. To stop and talk to a milkmaid in Grosvenor Square is a test of moral courage which I was prepared to undergo; but it might have compromised poor Kitty's unsullied reputation: so after one and two enquiries about her, made by me without looking at her (vile subterfuge!) and answered by her from behind, I walked away, and Kitty descended into the area of Lord Tom Noddy's house.

Saturday 11 June 1864. A day or two ago, M'Lean sent me two photographs of Sims's milkwoman: so excellent and so typical, that I insert one of them here, to illustrate and justify my much speaking about milkwomen. Look at this one: she is an English girl, about twenty seven years old, unmarried: look at her strong figure (though she is *not* one of the strongest) her homely easy attitude, her large solid feet, her large brown shapely hands; observe how the thick harness and heavy yoke sit home upon her shoulders; note the comfortable grace, the picturesque neatness, the utter freedom from fashion, of her rustic dress: she is one who lives in the heart of London, and yet can be like this! She is one who knows how to carry milk and scour pails, and probably knows little else; and yet, with all this, look at her face, how full of beauty it is – of sweet expression, of noble sincerity, of calm strength and modest self-reliance. To me, in her degree and kind she is altogether charming.

Thursday 27 July 1865. In the Adelphi yesterday, I saw a stout milklass walking along between her cans. Two boys, seeing her thus loaded, threw something at her from behind, and hit her. She said nothing, did not even turn round: but quietly set down her pails, hooked her harness together across her breast, and strode after them as they fled. In five yards she overtook the hindmost; boxed his ears without speaking a word; returned to her cans, and went on her way.

Thursday 1 February 1872. Went up to Baker Street and the Marylebone Road at 5. On Sunday . . . I passed in that road a photographer's frame full of pictures; and looking there, as my manner is, for portraits of working folk, I was agreeably surprised to see a 'carte de visite' of a milkwoman, wearing her yoke and pails: a thing I never saw in such place before. I went upstairs into the artist's den. 'Oh yes' said he 'I have several milkwomen; they often come to be taken, especially those who serve me'. And he produced half a dozen negatives. 'That's the old lady', he said, showing one of a stout cleanly dame, standing between her pails, with her harness hooked together across her breast; 'and that's Joanna', also a strong stout honest-looking woman, whose yoke was slung slantwise across her back; 'and that's Mary' – a quiet largehanded wench of thirty or so; and 'that's Young Mary'. 'They're all from Stoat's Dairy in Gloucester Place.' Now Young Mary, whose picture I had seen in the street, was the most striking of all. A robust but most feminine maiden, in the typical dress of her calling; in green plaid shawl, and pink cotton apron, and short stuff frock, and large stout ankleboots, and a red woollen kerchief tied over her old bonnet and framing the soft outline of her sweet and comely face: a face grave and tender, almost pensive; yet full of health and rustic vigour. Such is Young Mary; and in her picture she is taken just as you may see her in the streets; with her heavy beechen yolk on her shoulders, and the harness hanging taut on each side of her, with its large brass hooks and buckles; and her bare strong hands steadying the handles of the two great brassbound cans that swing full of milk against her skirts. A charming portrait of a working lass, as womanly as she is laborious.

I told the man to print them all; and called today to fetch them. there is no decay of female labour in the milktrade here, at any rate; 'they're *all* women about here, that carry milk', he said.

6: Female Gymnasts

Thursday 14 August 1862. I dined at the Oxford [Music Hall]: and enquiring there after the fate of one of the 'trapezists', who fell the other night while performing, the head waiter, an intelligent man, assured me that the proprietor of that place and of 'Canterbury Hall' did his best at first to provide good music and refined amusement, and so avoid the necessity of employing such persons; but that the rage of the public for their feats of senseless daring was so great that he was obliged to give in. The waiter himself expressed great contempt for this popular taste.

Monday 7 September 1868. I observed just opposite the Shoreditch Station a brilliantly lighted entrance to a 'Temperance Music Hall'. The admission was only *one penny*; and I went in, and found myself in the pit of a small and very dingy theatre, with a narrow stage. The pit was crowded, with people of the lowest class; chiefly costergirls and lads, in their working clothes. There was no drinking nor smoking, as in the grander Music Halls; both, indeed, were forbidden. Rough as they looked, the audience were quiet and well-behaved, and two policemen kept strict order. When I entered, a man and a lad were on the stage, drest in tights as acrobats, and performing in a humbler fashion and on one trapéze, hung low, feats such as I had just seen.* The lad seemed to be about ten years old; a sturdy wellknit little fellow, with broad shoulders, and a round plump smiling face, and curly hair parted on one side. He showed both pluck and skill; he climbed the rope, and hung from the trapéze by one hand or one foot, and sat astride his master's shoulder, and let himself be tossed and tumbled about, as the manner of street acrobats is with their young ones. There was nothing weak or feminine about the boy; but remembering how many female acrobats there are just now, I asked a girl who stood next me in the crowd – a shabbily drest but decent workgirl – whether the young performer were a boy or a girl. 'It's a *girl*, Sir!' she answered briskly; and added 'She's only been at it three weeks, besides 8 days, that she practised at home. Who is she? Well, they call her The little Azella;† but her name's Betsy Asher, and she's a Jewess, and only nine years old.' You know her then? 'She's my little sister, Sir', said the girl, proudly; 'and that's her mother and brother' – pointing to a woman and a young man, who sat just before us, gazing with delight at the feats of their athletic little girl. 'Oh yes', she went on, 'she likes it; she's took to it wonderful! Mother didn't want her to, but she begged hard, and so now she's 'prenticed to that gentleman for a twelve-month, for to learn her profession.' ‡Then does she mean to stick to it, and be an acrobat when she grows up? 'Oh yes, I believe so! You see Sir,' continued Miss Asher, 'it's quite the fashion for women now; why, there's Miss Foster at the Rising Sun, you know, she's took

ADOLPHE BEAU.   293, REGENT STREET.

Miss Murray. Miss Murray is (I am told) an American actress, who played in London in 1868. Comparing the face with the posture, this picture seems to me the most disgusting example of self degradation in a woman, that I have met with. Bought 1869.
Carte by Adolphe Beau of Regent Street, London.

*Earlier that evening Munby had watched Zuleilah – 'a Miss Foster, a publican's daughter of the neighbourhood' – perform on the trapeze at the Cambridge Music Hall. Munby explained in his diary that he was investigating such performances 'with a view to a paper on Female Gymnasts'.
†Azella was then the star attraction at the Holborn Amphitheatre.
‡She was apprenticed to a man calling himself 'M. de Vigne'. Girl acrobats could earn huge sums of money. Munby noted that a girl named Nathalie was being paid £80 a week for her performance in 1862.

Leona Dare, a Spanish American female acrobat, aged 24, performing at the Oxford Music Hall London, November 1878.

Saw her hang by her feet head downwards from the trapeze, and in that posture hold a strong man (by his waistband) in her teeth. Carte by Emile Tourtin of Paris.

Francello (Miss Palser?), English Female Acrobat of Bristol, aged 18, Nov. 1868. Carte by Holborn of Bristol.

Elizabeth Atkinson, aged 24, a Calcutta Eurasian. Carte by I. Preston of Leeds.

to it and she's performing every night at the Cambridge.' And your little sister really likes to climb and tumble about in this way, like a lad? 'Well, I only know she says so; and she practises hard enough!' Does she like *that*? I asked; for just then little Betsy, who was balancing on the trapéze, flung herself boldly off, as if taking a header, and swept head downwards along the inverted figure of her master, who was hanging by his heels. He caught her in her descent, by the ankles, and so she hung, head downwards. Does she like that? 'Yes!' said Miss Asher, emphatically, and gravely: 'she says that's one of the prettiest tricks of all!' And she looked calmly, as did her mother at little Betsy hanging so, in her tights and spangles.

Saturday 11 June 1870. Went round by the Oxford Music Hall, to see another female acrobat, soi-disant Md^{lle} de Glorion. She came forward to the footlights hand in hand with two male acrobats; she was drest much like them; and she made a bow, and not a curtsy, to the spectators, as they did.

A very pretty English girl, she seemed to be, of 18 or 20 years; trim and slight and shapely, standing about 5 feet 4. The only clothing she had on was a blue satin doublet fitting close to her body and having very scanty trunk hose below it. Her arms were all bare; her legs, cased in fleshings, were as good as bare, up to the hip: the only sign of a woman about her was that she had a rose in her bosom, and another in her short curly hair. . . . The

Female Cyclist, *1870.*
Carte by Ch. Reutlinger.

Mdlle Geraldine, Champion Lady
Gymnast. *1868.*
Carte by D. Daniels of Islington, London.

Azella, 1868. 'Azella' is (I am told) a
French colonial, married, having ne child.
She performed at the Holborn Amphitheatre
in 1868–9, and was rapturously applauded.
Carte taken for the London Stereoscopic
Company.

'chairman' got up and said 'Ladies and Gentlemen, Md^lle^ de Glorion will now take her daring leap for life, along the whole length of the hall.' And the fair acrobat went down from the stage among the audience, alone, and walked, halfnude as she was, through the crowd, to the other end of the long hall, and there went up a staircase into the gallery. She passed close by me; taking no heed of any one; her fair young face all crimson with heat and wet with perspiration; and climbed the rope ladder that led up from the gallery to a small platform, just big enough to stand on, which was suspended high up under the ceiling. There she stood, in sight of all the people; intent on preparing for her nightly peril, and taking no thought (nor did they, I

think, just then) of the fact that she was almost utterly unclothed. Two strong parallel ropes were stretched from hooks in the roof, fifty feet off, to the platform where she was: on the stage, far beyond that, one of her mates was hanging inverted from the trapéze, awaiting her; but he was wholly hidden from her by two great discs of paper stretched on hoops, which were hung near him, one behind the other, above the footlights. And she had to swing herself, high over the heads of the crowd, across that great space of eighty feet or so, and leap through the two discs and alight in his inverted arms, which she could not even see. A fair girl of eighteen, preparing in sight of all men for such a feat as that; perched up there, naked and unprotected,

*Mme. Senyah, i.e. Elizabeth Haynes. 1868.
Carte* taken for the London Stereoscopic
Company.

*Mme. Senyah, young English woman of 26:
as seen every night in London. 1868.
Carte* taken for the London Stereoscopic
Company.

with no one to help her; anxiously testing the ropes, chalking the soles of her feet, wiping the sweat off her hands and her bonny face, and trying to smile withal. One must suppose that if she had not been an acrobat, every man present would have rushed to rescue or assist her: as it was, she had hired herself to do the thing, and they sat still to see her do it. She did it, of course; she leaped into the air, and in leaping, left the ropes that swung her, and dashed through the two hoops, and was seen hanging in the arms of her mate, grasping his body, her face against his breast. A moment more, and she had lowered herself by the loose rope to the stage, and was bowing and smiling amidst thunders of applause. And so I came away.

Ought we to forbid her to do these things? Certainly not, if she wishes to do them and if *men* may do them unforbidden: the woe is with those by whom such offences come. And, though it is not well to see a nude man fling a nude girl about as she is flung, or to see her grip his body in mid air between her seemingly bare thighs, I think that an un-reflecting audience takes no note of these things and looks on him and her only as two performers. Still, the familiar interlacing of male and female bodies in sight of the public, is gross and corrupting, though its purpose be mere athletics.

Monday 6 February 1871. My object in going to the Holborn Circus was, to see a new female acrobat, calling herself *Lulu*, who has appeared there. Two years ago, the town was full of female acrobats; and I saw and de-scribed most of them, making the acquaint-ance of one or two, to see what manner of women such phenomena might be. Of late however, the 'Flying Ladies' and 'Lady Gymnasts' have only appeared at provincial Music Halls: in London, their robust feats have been eclipsed by the licensed strumpetry of the Cancan.

a

b

c

a) *Zazel – 'The Human Cannon Ball', as the advertisements call her – and the cannon out of which she has been fired twice daily ever since the 2nd. of April last, 14 May 1877.* Carte taken for the London Stereoscopic Company.

b) *'Zazel', an English Girl of 18, a Miss Dunn: a tight rope walker and acrobat: who appeared in public for the first time in April 1877, at the Westminster Aquarium: where twice a day, she walks the rope and performs feats thereon, and then swings on the high trapéze and leaps from it, and finally inserts herself into the mouth of a cannon, and is fired out of it into the air.*

After which, you may see her, in neat woman's clothing, quietly walking home along the street, carrying her little brother in her arms. 20 April 1877. Carte taken for the London Stereoscopic Company.

c) Lulu, *March 1871. 'Lulu' is an acrobat, now performing and turning somersaults with great success at the Holborn Amphitheatre.* Carte taken for the London Stereoscopic Company.

7: Maids-of-all-Work

The general servant, or maid-of-all-work, is perhaps the only one of her class deserving of commiseration: her life is a solitary one, and, in some places, her work is never done. . . . the mistress's commands are the measure of the maid-of-all-work's duties.

Beeton's Book of Household Management, (1861).

I went out to service too soon – before I really understood the meaning of it ' – & at the charity school i was taught to curtsy to the ladies & gentlemen, & it seem'd to come natural to me to think them entirely over the lower class & as if it was our place to bow & be at their bidding, & I've never got out o'that feeling somehow – I must leave it to others to judge whether I am the better or worse for it.

from the diary of Hannah Cullwick, maid-of-all-work,
Tuesday 30 September 1873.*

French servant girl *circ. 1860*.
Albumen print by A. Bilordeaux.

Wednesday 23rd December/63. i got up early & lighted the kitchen fire to get it up soon for the roasting – a turkey & eight fowls for tomorrow being Christmas Eve & forty people's expected & they're going to have a sort o play, and so they are coming tonight to do it over & the Missis has order'd a hot supper for 15 people – very busy indeed all day & worried too with the breakfast & the bells ringing so & such a deal to think about as well as work to do – i clean'd 2 pairs o boots & the knives – wash'd the breakfast things up – clean'd the passage & shook the door mat – got the dinner & clear'd away after – keeping the fire well up & minding the things what was roasting & basting em till i was nearly sick wi the heat & smell – the waiter came at 5 o'clock – i made the coffee & that & give the waiter it as he come for it up to 7 o'clock – Fred Crook came in & help'd me & i was glad of him as well as for company – we got the supper by a ¼ to ten, & we run up & down stairs to see some of the acting – just in the passage, & saw em all in their kings & queen's dresses – The queen of Spain was Miss Head & she come & spoke to me & i answer'd her 'Madam' & she laugh'd. we laid the kitchen cloth & had our supper & clear'd away after – i took the ham & pudding up at 12 o'clock – Made the fire up & put another on & then to bed – came down again at 4 for the wait's† woke me just in time – the fire wanted stirring

*At Munby's insistence, Hannah kept a diary for many years, and all the extracts in this section are taken from her diary entries, or from Munby's diary quoting her.
†'The waits' were informal groups of musicians and singers who went from house to house at Christmas and the New Year, playing and singing carols. Their traditional activities extended into the early hours of the morning. The traditional song *The Waits*, which dates back several centuries, has as its refrain: 'Past three o'clock! And a cold frosty morning, Past three o'clock! Good-morrow masters all!'

& morecoals on & when i'd got the pudding boiling again i went to bed till after six – got up & dress'd myself then & clean'd the tables & hearth & got the kettle boiling & so begun *Thursday* [Christmas Eve] – after breakfast i clean'd a pair o boots & lighted the fires up stairs – swept & dusted the room & the hall – laid the cloth for breakfast & took it up when the bell rung – put the beef down to roast – clean'd the knives – made the custards & mince pies – got the dinner up – clear'd away after & wash'd up in the scullery – clean'd the kitchen tables & hearth – made the fire up again & fill'd the kettle – made the coffee – wash'd myself a bit & put a clean apron on & give the waiters the coffee & milk as they ask'd for it – Fred Crook came in again & help'd me with the dishes & knives – we had supper in the kitchen & then i dish'd up for the parlour – lots o sweets came from Carter's & the jellies, & the man dish'd em up – we went up stairs & stood in the dining room door case & saw the acting in the other room – Mr Sanderson the cardinal came & spoke to us servants & was going to shake hands but i said 'my hands are dirty sir'. There was 4 singers the master got in for the night, so i ran up & listen'd to em & they sung capitally i think. after supper was over the Master had the hot mince pie up wi a ring & sixpence in it – they had good fun over it, cause Mr Grant got the ring & a young lady the sixpence – we had no fun downstairs, all was very busy till 4 o'clock & then to bed.

Friday Christmas day – Got up at eight & lit the fires – took the drugget* up & shook it &

laid it down again in the dining room – rubb'd the furniture & put straight – had my breakfast – clean'd a pair o boots – wash'd the breakfast things up & the dishes – clean'd the front steps – took the breakfast up stairs – got the dinner & fill'd the skuttles – the family went up the Hill for the evening & i clean'd myself to go & see Ellen† but i'd such a headache & felt so tired & sleepy – i sat in a chair & slept till five & then had tea & i felt better – it was a beautiful moonlight night & i walk'd up to the Grove & sat with them servants – had a little supper & home again & to bed at ten.

Saturday [Boxing Day] i lighted the fires & black'd the grates – the kitchen grate was so greasy i'd to wash it over first – i felt glad the Christmas was over so far for if it kept on long as it's bin the last 3 or 4 days i should be knock'd up i think.‡ i clean'd 2 pairs o boots – swept & dusted the room & the hall & got the breakfast up – The Missis came down into the kitchen & look'd round at what was left, & paid me my quarters wages – She saw i'd a missletoe hanging up & i told her ther'd bin no one kiss'd yet. She gave me the money for the Christmas boxes to the men & boys same as last year & give em as they came – i got a lot too – near two lbs in all – they was sent to me – Mr Grant 3 & 4d & Mr Saunderson the same – Mr Hons 5 shillings & old Mrs Foster 2 & 6d – the rest was from the tradesmen – i put mine in the bank wi my wages, Mary says hern shall buy a new bonnet. i clean'd the kitchen & passage & the stairs & wash'd up in

A Housemaid: servant in a gentleman's family near Twyford. Taken (by her own desire) at Twyford, August 1873. Carte by an unidentified photographer.

*A coarse woollen floor-covering.
†Hannah's sister.
‡No wonder Hannah feared that she might get 'knock'd up' – she had slept for only four hours on Christmas Eve and just over five hours the night before. Even then she had to get up in the early hours to get the pudding boiling and tend the fire. As almost every waking hour was spent working, the general servant or maid-of-all-work had to be a hardy creature – a reliable consumer durable in human form: 'No machine, even of American invention, can bear comparison with this old-fashioned one either for simplicity, efficacy, or durability. Its construction involves the use of neither iron, nor brass, nor steel: valves, cranks, and cogs are not material to its economy. Though composed of only flesh and blood and bone it is tougher than hammered iron; it seldom gets out of order, rarely blows up, and, more important than all, it consumes an amazing small amount of fuel.'[1]

Country Servant Girl, aged about 24. Westminster Road, 1862. 'She had come to London to see the Exhibition. Her hands were very large, coarse, and red, as if she'd done rare hard work: and she seemed proud of them.'

Per H. Dunning, Photographer.

Ambrotype.

Maid of all work. Aldgate. Taken 1861. Ambrotype by an unidentified photographer.

Servant. Oxford Street. Taken 1861. Ambrotype by an unidentified photographer.

the scullery – got the supper over & to bed at ten.

Sunday January 1st /71. This is the beginning of another year, & i am still general servant like, to Mrs Henderson at 20 Gloucester Crescent [Paddington, London]. this month on the 16th i shall o' bin in her service 2 years & a ½, & if i live till the 26th o' May when i shall be 38 years old; i shall o' bin in service 30 years & have known Massa 17 years. Now there's such a little boy kept here i've a deal more to do – of jobs that's hard, like digging coals & carrying 'em up & the boxes, & high windows & the fan light over the door to clean & anything as wants strength or height i am sent for or call'd up to do it, all the cabs that's wanted i get, & if the young ladies want fetching or taking anywhere i've to walk with them & carry their cloaks or parcels. i clean all the copper skuttles & dig the coals – clean the

tins & help to clean the silver & do the washing up if i'm wanted, & carry things up as far as the door for dinner – i clean 4 grates & do the fires & clean the irons – sweep & clean 3 rooms & my attic – the hall & front steps & the flags & area railings & all that in the street – i clean the water closet & privy out & the back yard & the area – the back stairs & the passage – the larder, pantry & boy's room – & the kitchen & scullery – all the cupboards down stairs & them in the storeroom – & at the housecleaning i do the walls down from top to the bottom o' the house & clean all the high paint, & dust the pictures. I get all the meals down stairs & lay the cloth & wait on the boy & the housemaid, as much as they want & if it's my work, like changing their plates & washing their knife & fork & that. Missis never goes away – hardly for a day throughout the year, so as there's no change and no good chance for thorough cleaning

Maid of all work. Dartford. Taken 1861.
Ambrotype by an unidentified
photographer.

Servant c. 1856–61.
Ambrotype by an unidentified
photographer.

Maid of all work. City. Taken 1856.
Ambrotype by an unidentified
photographer.

but i'm getting more used to the family now so i don't mind them seeing me clean up stairs so much as i used to, but i do like the family to be away for housecleaning, cause one can have so much more time at it & do it more thoroughly & be as black at it as one likes without fear o'bein seen by the ladies, cause i know they don't like to see a servant look dirty however black the job is one has to do.

i've had two days & two nights holiday since last October twelve months, & bin to no theatres or Crystal Palace or anything except to Exeter Hall once wi the young ladies & heard the ragged school children sing – And i've read nothing but a book call'd Adam Bede, except in my Bible – i've bin to church every chance i've had when Massa's bin away or when i've not gone to him of a Sunday – it's rather unpleasant to ask leave so i seldom get out of a weekday. i go with notes or parcels, & fetch my beer or for any

errands, yet i get very little outing all together – the most fresh air is washing the front door steps & flags in the street & out at the back door washing the yard. Still, i'm quite content & like service – especially if i could get to Massa more & without having to ask – but that i canna so am obliged to make the best of the time i do have & do as much in it as i can for him. And this year i pray that i may do better nor ever i've done afore – that i may *understand* & have spirit & a will to do all that's right, & that i may be happy – & that is when i please my Master. . . .

i wear the same black straw bonnet as i've had for years & my plaid or grey shawl generally – i sleep in the attic still, & find it very cold this weather – i do my hair & wash in the scullery every day – Saturday Nights i wash by the fire in the bucket as i clean with.[2]

Wednesday 10th May /71. i got up early – did

Maid of all work, at a coffee house in Bermondsey! Taken 1861.
Ambrotype by an unidentified photographer.

Maid of all work. Dartford. Taken 1861.
Ambrotype by an unidentified photographer.

Maidservant. Edgeware Road, 1863.
Ambrotype by an unidentified photographer.

the sweeping & clean'd the hall & watercloset on my knees before breakfast – shook the mats – wash'd me & got our breakfast – did the dusting after, & to prayers at 9 – wash'd up & clean'd the hearth – put straight & dusted the potboard on my knees – Miss M[argaret] give orders for an early dinner, & give me the things out in the storeroom,* but i wouldn't ax leave of her, to go out, cause the last time i did she scrupled, & said she would ask Missis Henderson, but never give me any answer – so when Missis was alone in the dining room afore the dinner went up, i tidied myself & knock'd at the parlour door & went in – i ask'd if i may go out, & Missis said, 'What's going on tonight? i don't think the ladies are going out to want you – *Yes*, if you can manage for tea' – i said 'Yes Mam, i can fry the fish afore i go' – She said, very well, & i said 'thank you mam' & come down again, pleas'd enough that the asking part was over, what i always *do* so dislike, & i finish'd getting the dinner, & after ourn i was having my sit, when Miss Margaret call'd me up to her in the storeroom, & said, 'Oh, will tomorrow do for you to go out instead of today? i said '*NO Mam* it won't', at once, cause i knew M[assa] wouldn't be in & this was the only day he could see me, & besides it was thrown too late for me to send him word, & i wouldn't disappoint *him* any how if i could help it, so perhaps i was a bit hasty – Well, Miss M. says

*Three weeks previously Hannah had complained in her diary about Miss Margaret's tight control of the storeroom: 'every little thing i've to ax for & i *canna* always remember at the time what i may want to use & so it's inconvenient – besides i think it shows so little trust & treating a servant like a child – so i don't like the plan.'

Housemaid. Westminster Bridge Road.
Taken 1861.
Ambrotype by an unidentified
photographer.

Servant. Lambeth. Taken 1861.
Ambrotype by an unidentified
photographer.

Maid of all work. Westminster Bridge Road.
Taken 1861.
Ambrotype by an unidentified
photographer.

'*Why* won't tomorrow do,' & look'd rather proud – i said, 'because it's too late to alter it now Mam, & i've made the appointment' – she said, 'You've no right to make appointments without first knowing whether you can be spar'd'. then i said how i always waited for the orders in a morning & if there was a late dinner or anything to keep me back i never ask'd, nor i didn't *wish* to leave my work, but i'd bin hard at work yesterday & baking & that, & busy again getting forward this morning, & so today suited me best for going out, that tomorrow i sh^d have bread to bake again perhaps, & i couldn't leave that – Miss M. said she was the best judge of that, & i said 'No Mam, you canna tell about my work so well as i can', & i suppose she saw a little temper in me, the same as i saw in her, for she said – '*Hannah* you forget your place' – i said '*No Mam i dont*, but it puts me out after i've got

leave, & put straight, to be stopp'd for nothing.' Miss M. said, 'Well, there's no need for me to tell you what it's for if you can't alter it, but things can't go on like this' – i said 'No Mam they can't', & i come down stairs feeling very angry & vex'd. Bye & bye Missis rang for me into the dining room, & said that as i'd bin so insolent to Miss Margaret she thought 'twas best for her & me to part. i said 'Very well Mam, & i hope you'll stick to it, & not ask me to stop on as you did before, for i've got a hard place of work, but that i *like*. it's what i've to bear from Miss M. what i don't like, & she's very mean in the housekeeping.' i come out feeling very much annoy'd but not sorry, for i felt that for a good many reasons it would be a good thing, having never bin in the country now for nearly 3 years, & never dare ask for a night or a day even so as to give one time to clean or turn round for a bit o' sewing

Hannah, 1864.
Carte by J. Stodart of Margate.

& that – still the disagreeable feel of throwing oneself out o' place & searching for a new one come up & made it unpleasant.*

Friday 12th May /71. after prayers Missis order'd me to be at Dr Grave's by 11 to fetch Miss Forrest home from a party – Missis says it's not respectable for me to be out after ten & yet she sent me there at 11 o'clock. i knock'd at the door & said 'i'm come for Miss Forrest please,' & the servant said 'come in, & sit down', & i did, on a bench in the hall what's meant for servants & poor folks to wait on. It was a large grand looking house outside with two entrances like & lots o' flowers in the garden – two or 3 lamps lighted up, & there seem'd to be two biggish halls, & the stairs as led to the drawing room i could see, & so i could see the ladies & gentlemen come down & go up from the supper, & i couldn't get out o'sight either – had my milkwoman's bonnet on – a cotton frock & white apron – my cloak on & a white comforter round my neck, so i look'd rough to go for a lady – And the servant as let me in must of told about me, for all the women servants come one after another & walk'd round & look'd but never spoke to me – i expected them too & made a move as if to speake but they didn't, & i leant my head again the wall again to sleep if i could & just listen to the music, for i could hear it quite plain, & some singing was going on too – i was pleas'd to hear it all, & i see the ladies come down arm'd by the gentlemen – & the ladies was so grandly dress'd, with their dresses dragging after them more than a yard i sh[d] think, & sticking out so behind, they looked loaded. Then i noticed how proud some of 'em look'd & how polite & smiling the gentlemen was to them, & i thought – 'i suppose that's how Massa does among the ladies,' & i fancied as if he was one o' them coming down – But i didn't feel a bit *jealous*, & i wouldn't o' changed places wi' them ladies neither not for worlds, & so i told M. afterwards – still, i liked to see 'em & think of *him*, like he thinks of *me* when he sees servants doing rough work like mine. A gentleman brought Miss Forrest at last, & i got up & curtsied & open'd the door – *he* never noticed me, but Miss Forrest give me her shoes to carry & said 'i hope you've not bin waiting long,' & i said only ½ an hour Mam,' & i follow'd her out – i'd to show her the way back – it was a pleasant night & she would walk by my side & talk'd quite free. & as we stood under the lamp at our door she star'd up into my face – She is pretty, & i reckon wanted me to look at her.

Thursday 15th June /71. i made gooseberry cheese. & after the dinner i turn'd the rubbish drawer out – put the rags together & took 'em to the shop – sold them for 5[d.], that pays for 5½ pints of beer, or more nor a weeks tea, for i find both myself.†

Tuesday 25th July /71. i was down at lunch, & one o' the carpenters pretended to admire me rather – he praised my arm for being so big, &

*The incident blew over, though not before Hannah had tried to explain to Munby 'how it was to feel – a great big wench & strong as i am, as could *crush* a weak thing like Miss Margaret is, with one hand, (tho of course i *wouldn't*) & she must know that – for her to *trifle* with me about going out, when i'd got leave too – & *play* with me as if i was a child & unkindly too.' Hannah's 'Missis' and her daughter 'Miss M.' were worried that her relationship with a mysterious gentleman friend was perhaps not perfectly respectable. After Hannah's marriage all was explained and she returned with Munby to visit Mrs. Henderson and Miss Margaret, who were very friendly towards her.

†Board and lodging was free for a domestic servant; the wages paid sometimes included an allowance of beer, tea and sometimes sugar. Hannah's wages would have been slightly more because she had to 'find' these items for herself. Oddments such as rags, dripping, and cinders were regarded – below stairs at least – as 'perks' which brought in a useful few pence. Hannah used to drink two half pints of beer a day '& was the better for it'.

made such flattering & winning speeches like, as he leant on the table, till i was quite tickled, & couldn't help laughing at him – i said '*Pray be quiet* – i don't understand all that,'& i told him how old i was [38] but he didn't seem to believe it, & ask'd me if he should come on Sunday to go out with me – i said 'Oh *certainly*', but it was only my fun – then while the others was up wi the pictures he came down again with some excuse & begun talking again, & come up to me & tried to kiss me, but i said 'i never allow anybody to kiss me' – then he said i was wasting all my best days' i said 'never mind, *i* don't'. He tried again to kiss me & i push'd him away & run round the kitchen table, & him after me till i thought it was beginning to look silly, & i run up stairs to my work, & i see no more of him till the afternoon & i was cleaning a fender in one o' the rooms – he come in for a duster & begun his nonsense again – i said 'now look at my hands, they're pretty black, & if you touch me i'll stroke your face with 'em so you'd better be quiet,' & i chased him down stairs to the others in the drawing room – they did laugh so, & egg'd me on to black his face – he was afraid i should, but i didn't for i meant him no harm & i didn't want to offend him, but i let him see that i didn't want *him* either, & when he went away he shook hands with me & said he supposed he sh^d never see me again, & i said 'perhaps not but it's no matter if you never do.' There was something so absurd about the man seeming to like *me*, that i was more amused than anything else, & it's so unusual for anyone to praise me in my dirt except M[assa] that i never look for it – indeed i always take it for granted that i'm look'd down on & despised. it made little difference to me whether this man meant what he said or not – perhaps he did & perhaps he didn't.

Ladies is so fiddle faddle . . . and so finikin, and so mincing and affected: you don't know where to have 'em, nor what they mean hardly. Eh, Miss Margaret used to aggravate

Hannah Cullwick.
General servant to Mr. Jackson, a tradesman, at Kilburn.
About 1860.
Ambrotype by an unidentified photographer.

Hannah, 1867.
Carte by O. G. Rejlander.

Hannah, 1867.
Carte by O. G. Rejlander.

Hannah, 1867.
Carte by O. G. Rejlander.

me so! . . . her was so sighing-like and delicate, one couldn't speak plain to her nor understand her. Once, I ax'd her if us servants might have cabbage for our dinner – it was Emily and me, you know; and her says, 'What for? Why do you want cabbage?' Well, I give her a hint, this way and that, but she could'nt take it; so at last I says, 'Well Ma'am, you know as cabbage is good to open the bowels'. 'Oh Hannah', she says, 'how can you speak like that to *me?*'' 'Well Ma'am', I says, 'I meant no harm I'm sure, only you won't let one speak to be understood!' And then her cried over it, and *I* cried to see *her* cry: and all about a bit o' cabbage!³

Sunday 22nd January 1871. i could go on for a long time about things i remember in all them years and the different places i was at, & the many sorts of fellow servants i've lived with,

& i like to think of them past years, still, it seems to me hardly worth talking about a poor servant's life like mine, but Massa likes me to talk & write about it, & since it's all i know, it's nice that he *does* like it.

Tuesday 30th September 1873. This is the last day o' the month, & Massa only wishes me to write to the end – and I am glad of it somehow, for I've got so thoroughly tired o' writing what i think to most people must be very tiresome & certainly *disinteresting*. I hardly think i shᵈ care to read *one lady's* diary of twenty years standing tho' of course theirn would be more varied than a servants can possibly be. And so i've told M. that by making me write for so many years he has quite tired me of it, & yet for some things I am most glad that he's not tired of reading it.

III: 'WOMAN'S RIGHTS'

BY ARTHUR MUNBY

One must take the rough with the smooth.

*Nec crimen duras esset habere manus.**

---

*'And it was no crime to have horny hands.' Ovid, *Fasti*, III, 782.

□ *Carte* portraits of tip girls taken by
W. Clayton of Tredegar, *c.* 1865.

'Woman's Rights'

Some say, that women should be weak;
That sunburnt throat and roughen'd cheek
   Are wholly out of place
For that sweet sex, whose duty lies
In having lovely lips and eyes,
   And attitudes all grace.

And some, with difference, are agreed
That women should be weak, indeed,
   Of body and of limb;
But, *en revanche*, in brain and mind
They may and ought to be a kind
   Of stronger seraphim.

Weak? cries another; why, they are!
No talk of 'should be:' you're aware
   That much diversity
Of ways, of frame, and, in a word,
Of nature, makes it quite absurd
   For them to work as we.

'Of course!' says one; 'it's not our trade:
Our little hands were never made
   To wipe another's dust;
So here's the formula I use:
"Let women work because they choose,
   And men because they must."

'That is, at handiwork. But brains!
I shall not waste (says she) much pains
   To prove and prove again
That women needn't stay at home
To use them; they may go and come,
   A better sort of men,

'At mart and meeting, church and bar:
Wherever fame and fortune are
   There I (she says) believe
That women shortly will resort;
Till every Adam finds in court
   An opposition Eve.'

Alas, my lively learned friends!
This child but feebly comprehends
   The meaning of it all:
What with your speeches and your sections,
Your arguments and grave objections,
   Your – well, I won't say gall;

Your pamphlets, letters to the *Times*,
Smart magazines, and ready rhymes
   On everything but love;
And papers too by high-soul'd men,
Whose bosoms bleed for Lydia, when
   She soils her dainty glove;

I tell you, what with this and that,
We plain ones can't think what you're at;
   Indeed we really can't:
And therefore, in the name of sense,
Eschew negation and pretence,
   And say the thing you want!

Look here: you strive, and nobly too,
To find employment for that crew
   Of hapless imbeciles
(Excuse the word) whose lot in life
Lies 'twixt the needle and the knife,
   Unless they sell their smiles:

You trust them with a watch's works;
You make them prentices and clerks;
   Put pens behind their ears;
Or bid them tell the feeling cords,
In vivid music of dumb words,
   Our triumphs and our fears:

'Tis new; but who will interfere?
For me, I trust that every year
   Your telegraphic maids,
Your girls who copy briefs and wills
Or set up circulars and bills,
   May flourish in their trades.

Et puis, mesdames? These quiet duties
May do for sedentary beauties;
   But, you yourselves must own,
All women don't like sitting still;
All are not competent to fill
   A clerkly seat in town.

Some lasses, neither slim nor fair,
Live mostly in the open air,
   And rather like it, too:
Their faces and their hands are brown;
Their fists, perchance, might knock you down,
   If they were minded to!

What say you then of such as these?
May they continue, if they please,
   To swing the pail, to scrub,
To make the cheese, to warm the cruds,
And lash the storm of steaming suds
   Within the washing-tub?

'Well, yes,' say you; 'undoubtedly:
We meddle not with them; you see
   Our business is with wrong;
We wish to set the balance straight,
And somewhat equalize in fate
   The feeble and the strong.

'We seek the *middle* classes' good:
Their overflowing womanhood
   Exactly suits our plan;
Which is, to prove the latent might
Of women, and assert their right
   To work abreast of man.'

Good: and a blessing on the deed!
Since then you're anxious to succeed,
   I gladly make it known
That Nature, in her wiser hours,
Has seconded this plan of yours
   By teachings of her own.

'Whene'er you take your walks abroad,'
You'll haply see along the road,
   In field, or yard, or farm,
Those girls of whom I spoke just now:
You'll see them lift a sweating brow,
   Or bare a rough red arm

Right up through all its brawny length;
And do with ease such feats of strength
   As make you ladies stare;
Or, pausing in their toil, they'll stand
And hold you out a harden'd hand,
   And ask you how you are.

Is it not comfort, then, to know
These wenches have such thews to show,
   And work with such a will?
What health there is in every face!
And, if with a Herculean grace,
   Are they not graceful still?

'Oh no!' you scream, 'good gracious, no!
You *wicked* man! How dare you so
   Distort our publish'd views?
We *hate* what is unfeminine;
We can't see anything divine
   In muscles or in thews!

'Hard hands! and oh, a dirty face!
What sad indelible disgrace
   For this soft sex of ours!
We want them to be nice and clean;
With tasteful dress and gentle mien,
   Like nymphs among the flowers!

'If those poor souls are so degraded
They fancy they can work, unaided
   By our wise counsellings,
We must, we really must, present
And pass a Bill through Parliament
   To stop such dreadful things!

'Why were they never, never taught
To scorn their labour as they ought,
   And feel that it is wrong
Thus to use strength and gain by it?
It doesn't signify one bit
   That they *are* well and strong:

'We're bound to *show* them what they want;
To say they mustn't and they shan't
   Destroy their fair complexions
By doing work that *men* should do:
Great, big, ungrateful men like you,
   Who raise these weak objections!'

I raise objections? Nay, my dears:
'Tis true, I've watch'd their work for years
   With no unfriendly eye;
Because, alas! in every point
My facts are somewhat out of joint
   With half your theory.

But now, you see, you're caught at last:
Women, whose powers are so vast,
   Are *children*, after all!
They mustn't give, as men may give,
Their sweat and brains, nor freely live
   In great things and in small:

They must be guided from above,
By quips of patronizing love,
   To do or not to do:
Though they be made of stalwart stuff,
Buxom and brave and stout enough,
   And full of spirit too,

Yet they may never seek, forsooth,
To enterprize their lusty youth
   In labours or commands
Which, while they leave unfetter'd course
To native energy and force,
   Might spoil their pretty hands!

'Nay, spoil their woman's heart,' say you.
What! Then you think it isn't true
   That every woman dims
The moon-like lustre of her kind
As much by manliness of mind
   As manliness of limbs?

Or else – and this is what you mean –
You simply seek a grander scene,
   A more sublime display,
For female talents of the brain:
You strive (I hope 'tis not in vain)
   To find your sex a way

To share our honours and our fame –
The civic or forensic name
   On which your fancy lingers;
But, when it comes to rough hard work,
You will not help us with a fork –
   Much less with your white fingers.

There is a game that schoolboys use,
Called 'Heads I win, and tails you lose;'
   And this smart game of shares,
Wherein we men are to be drudges,
And you both *élégantes* and Judges,
   Seems very much like theirs.

Why don't you drop it, and be frank?
For our part, we must say point-blank,
   With much respectful moan,
That we'll oppose you tooth and nail,
Unless you'll swallow *all* the whale,
   Or let the beast alone.

Either agree, you stand apart,
As much by nature as by art,
   In power of the mind –
In grasp of knowledge – in the right
Of work – in such inferior might
   As differs kind from kind;

Either confess (and Truth forbid
We should allow it, if you did)
   That you are born to serve:
Slight creatures, only fit to stand
The smaller tasks of head and hand:
   Weaklings in every nerve:

Or else, take heart of grace, and say,
'You men, we'll meet you any day
   On all the field of life;
Save only to our bounded sex
The matron care that guards and checks
   A mother, or a wife.'

Since there is work for all and each,
Rough or refined in frame and speech,
   Rudely or gently nurst, –
Take it; and if you need defence,
Cry, *Honi soit qui mal y pense*,
   And let them think their worst.

But don't come forth, with hand on hip
And such grand airs of championship
   To battle for your right,
And then turn round on half your troops
With these terrific howls and whoops,
   Because they love to fight

In ways less ladylike than yours:
Don't say your Amazons are boors,
   And mustn't seek to ride,
Because, when they have tighten'd girth.
Like half the women of the earth
   They choose to mount astride.

Don't practise, in your noble rage,
To stint an honest maiden's wage
   And dwarf her vigour too,
Whene'er her daily labours fall
'Mid scenes which you think bad for all,
   Because they startle *you*.

Weaklings, indeed! Yon stunted girl
Who minds the bobbins as they twirl
   Or plies the flashing loom,
She is a weakling, if you will:
And yet, because she works on still
   Shut up inside a room,

You let her work; you don't pretend
That *that* degrades her in the end:
   But, if she dares to go
And brace her muscles in the fields,
Till with a sinewy arm she wields
   The hayfork or the hoe,

Straight you lift up your prudish eyes,
Affect a feminine surprise,
   And do your best to spoil
The hearty health, the bluff content,
That Nature's righteous self hath sent
   To bless her sunburnt toil!

Weaklings? I chanced to be of late
Where young Tom Prentiss and his mate
   Were working side by side:
Who was his mate? *A woman*, dears!
A lass whom he has loved for years;
   His sweetheart, Ellen Hyde.

Ah, Ellen is a girl to see·
She has not sacrificed—not she—
   Her massive breadth of limb:
If any lad less kind and good
Than Tom, should happen to be rude,
   She'd make short work of him!

Yet with her strength she is most fair;
Fairest of all the women there,
   When summer morns are rathe
She seeks her labour, and her large
Lithe form is hail'd by every barge
   That lies along the staith.

Save the red beads about her neck
(Tom's gift) her beauty has no speck
   Of gawds and coquetries:
Her bonnet tilted o'er her brow
Is set there, not to guard its snow,
   But just to shade her eyes.

Beneath a sleeveless vest of say
Her ample shoulders freely play,
   Her bosom beats at ease;
And, veil'd by half her kilted gown,
The lindsey kirtle loiters down
   Not far below her knees.

Her hosen? Yes, their warm grey strands
Were knitted by her own true hands
   Beside the cottage fire;
And ankle-boots of size and weight,
Nail-studded, shoed with iron plate,
   Complete her brave attire.

Thus have I seen her ply her trade,
With Tom at hand to cheer and aid—
   Though aid she needed none:
Who should compare her frame with his
Might fairly doubt, if that or this
   Could better work alone:

And sometimes, when a pause was made,
Leaning on pickaxe or on spade
   She smiled and whisper'd low,
Whilst, with long labour grown too warm,
She drew her firm and freckled arm
   Across her beaded brow.

Thus too, within her mother's home
I've seen her frankly go and come—
   So bonny, and so tall;
And seen her sleek her chestnut hair,
And mend her things of workday wear,
   And smooth her Sunday shawl,

And sew, in hope of leisure hours,
Her bonnet with the wee bit flowers
   That Tom would most approve;
And in her broken looking-glass
Behold unmoved as sweet a lass
   As man could wish to love.

Ah Virtue, what a sight was here!
A sight for those to whom is dear
   The substance, not to show:
A woman strong to dare and do,
Yet soft towards suffering, and true
   In welfare and in woe:

Whose woman's nature is not lost,
Nor marr'd, nor even tempest-tost,
   But strengthen'd and controll'd:
Who, working thus with sinewy hands,
Grows deaf to Folly's fond commands,
   Grows calm and solemn-soul'd.

Yes, ladies of the Yankee creed,
We scruple not to see you bleed –
   With lancets – if you will,
Or show the pulpit and the bar
How worthy of ourselves you are
   In subtlety and skill;

But, leave your stronger mates alone:
They, tense of thews and stout of bone,
   Rejoice to work amain;
And so they shall, in breadth and length:
As free to use their woman's strength
   As you your woman's brain.

Notes

The number references – for example (Munby 33) – are to the numerical ordering of the Munby documents in the Library of Trinity College, Cambridge.

PART I

1: Working Women

Chapter heading quotation: Munby's diary, 19 July 1859. (Munby 2)
1. Munby's diary, Wednesday 5 June 1861. (Munby 8)
2. Munby's diary, ibid.
3. The statistics are taken from the article which accompanied du Maurier's illustrations: no author given, 'The Living Stream at London Bridge', *London Society*, Vol. III, 1863, pp. 214–15. The traffic census was taken on 16 March 1859, which was a Wednesday.
4. Munby's diary, Saturday 26 April 1862. (Munby 13)
5. From a letter signed 'A.J.M.', quoted in *The Wigan and District Advertiser*, Saturday 30 January 1886, p.2.
6. Munby's diary, Tuesday 19 July 1859. (Munby 2)
7. Munby's diary, Friday 27 May 1864. (Munby 25)
8. Munby's diary, Tuesday 23 February 1869. (Munby 37)
9. op. cit. (London, 1876), pp. 137–8. This chapter was originally published under the title 'London Courts and Alleys' in the *Standard*, August 1875.
10. Munby's diary, Saturday 8 February 1862. (Munby 12)
11. Munby's diary, Saturday 21 March 1863. (Munby 18)
12. Munby's diary, Friday 2 December 1870. (Munby 38)
13. Munby's diary, Wednesday 29 September 1869. (Munby 37)
14. Munby's diary, Monday 13 June 1864. (Munby 25)

2: 'Suggestive Contrasts'

Chapter heading quotation: Munby's diary, Friday 1 August 1862. (Munby 14)
1. Munby's diary, Wednesday 23 April 1862. (Munby 13)
2. Munby's diary, Monday 21 July 1862. (Munby 14)
3. No author given, 'Cœlebs in Search of a Mulready Envelope. A Liverpool Romance', *London Society*, Vol. VII, 1865, illustration facing p. 29. The title is based on Hannah More's *Cœlebs in Search of a Wife* (1809), which professed to be written by a young man looking for an ideal woman.
4. Munby's diary, Wednesday 3 July 1872. (Munby 40)
5. Munby's diary, Friday 11 May 1860. (Munby 5)
6. Munby's diary, Saturday 19 September 1868. (Munby 36) Munby had first met her in 1863.
7. Munby's diary, Friday 1 August 1862. (Munby 14)
8. Munby's diary, Friday 14 December 1860. (Munby 7)

9. See Munby's diary, Saturday 9 February 1867. (Munby 35)
10. Munby's diary, Friday 7 November 1860. (Munby 7)
11. An unsigned article, 'The Mechanical Sempstress', in *Once a Week*, 20 August 1864, p. 232, gave 8 hours 27 minutes as the time taken to make a silk dress by hand. This was contrasted with the speed of a steam-powered sewing machine which could produce the same article in 1 hour 13 minutes.
12. Quoted in an unsigned article, 'Needlewomen', in *The Social Science Review*, 1 February 1865; Vol. III, p. 108. The evidence quoted was collected by Mr. Lord, an Assistant Commissioner, and was incorporated in the *Second Report of the Children's Employment Commission* (1864).
13. Munby's diary, Wednesday 12 June 1861. (Munby 8)
14. From Munby's 'Visits to Hannah' Vol. X, entry dated Saturday 11 January 1890, pp. 116–22 (Munby 75). It is difficult to tell when this incident occurred. Munby mentions it in his diary entry for Monday 2 February 1863, saying it happened 'once, long ago'.
15. Munby's diary, Friday 10 July 1863. (Munby 19)
16. Hannah's diary, Friday 2 January 1863. (Munby 98[1])
17. Unsigned article, but by Eliza Lynn Linton, 'Mésalliances', *The Saturday Review*, 26 September 1868, Vol. XXVI, p. 419.
18. Munby's diary, Tuesday 13 May 1862. (Munby 13)
19. Munby's diary, Saturday 8 February 1862. (Munby 12)
20. Munby's diary, Wednesday 29 February 1860. (Munby 4)
21. John Duguid Milne, *Industrial Employment of Women in the Middle and Lower Ranks*, (revised edition, London, 1870, pp. 75–6; the first edition was published anonymously in 1857 with the title *Industrial and Social Position of Women in the Middle and Lower Ranks*).
22. 'My Duties Towards Society, By a Young Lady of the Period', stanzas VI and VII, published in *The Girl of the Period Miscellany*, No. 2, April 1869, p. 65. The writer signed himself 'Patricius. – T.C.D.'
23. Munby's diary, Saturday 16 August 1862. (Munby 14)
24. W. P. Frith, *My Autobiography and Reminiscences*, Vol. I (London, 1887), pp. 248–9. The girl was persuaded to sit for a painting to which he gave the title *The Sleepy Model*. This became Frith's diploma picture when he was elected a Royal Academician in 1853.
25. Note in Munby's diary for early 1860, dated 19 June 1894. (Munby 4)
26. Munby's diary, Tuesday 26 May 1863. (Munby 19)
27. Hannah's diary, Wednesday 26 April 1865. (Munby 98[3])
28. Munby's diary, Saturday 9 August 1862. (Munby 14)
29. Munby's diary, Sunday 19 January 1862. (Munby 12)
30. Hannah's diary, Saturday 30 August 1873. (Munby 98[7])
31. Munby's notebook with diary entries relating to their French tour; entry for Saturday 30 August 1873. (Munby 97[5])
32. Munby's notebook, Saturday 12 September 1874. (Munby 97[6])

33. Munby's diary, Sunday 4 March 1860. (Munby 4)
34. op. cit., first published 1762, quoted from the translation by Barbara Foxley in Everyman's Library (1966 reprinting), pp. 328 and 332.
35. Bessie Rayner Parkes, 'The Changes of Eighty Years', in *Essays on Woman's Work*, (London, 1865), pp. 47–9. She is quoting from Anna Seward's life of Erasmus Darwin: *Memoirs of the Life of Dr. Darwin, Chiefly During his Residence at Lichfield, with Anecdotes of his Friends, and Criticisms on his Writings*, (London, 1804). In his entry on Thomas Day in the *Dictionary of National Biography*, (London, 1888), Leslie Stephen warns that the details of these stories 'rest upon the very doubtful authority of Miss Seward' (Vol. XIV, p. 240). Anna Seward told how Mr. Day's search for an ideal wife originated:

> He resolved, if possible, that his wife should have a taste for literature and science, for moral and patriotic philosophy. *So* might she be his companion in that retirement, to which he had destined himself; and assist him in forming the minds of his children to stubborn virtue and high exertion. He resolved also, that she should be simple as a mountain girl, in her dress, her diet, and her manners; fearless and intrepid as the Spartan wives and Roman heroines. – There was no finding such a creature ready made; philosophical romance could not hope it. He must mould some infant into the being his fancy had imaged. (p. 35)

36. Undated manuscript by Munby, 'My Wife and her Friends', p. 15. (Munby 109¹)

3: Who Should Wear the Trousers?

Chapter heading quotations:
J. S. Mill, *The Subjection of Women*, (London, 1869), from the first section of Chapter 1 (p. 29 in the 1924 edition). The song is quoted by Stella Mary Newton in *Health, Art and Reason, Dress Reformers of the 19th century*, (London, 1974), pp. 4–5.
1. Munby's diary, Tuesday 19 January 1864. (Munby 23)
2. *Punch*, Vol. XXI, (1851), p. 34.
3. Munby's diary, Sunday 17 July 1859. (Munby 2)
4. Munby's diary, Monday 18 July 1859. (Munby 2)
5. *Punch*, Vol. XXI, (1851), p. 269 commented that this 'entirely put an end to the Bloomer fever', and J. C. Flugel in *The Psychology of Clothes* (London, 1930; fourth impression 1966) footnote on p. 152, describes this as a classic example of what he calls 'negative prestige': 'A fashion may be killed in its infancy by being adopted by persons whom it is considered undesirable to imitate.'
6. Unsigned article, 'The Woman's Dress Association', *The Saturday Review*, 24 February 1872, p. 245.
7. One should be careful not to make the Victorians seem completely unaware of their absurdities. At a time when the jobs of the Wigan pit brow girls were at risk, in part at least because they wore trousers, *The Saturday Review* (21 May 1887, p. 715) could see enough humour in the situation to entitle a serious article on the problem in 1887 'Pit Brows and Piano Legs'.
8. Munby's diary, Monday 2 February 1863. (Munby 17)
9. Unsigned article, 'Costume and its Morals', *The Saturday Review*, 13 July 1867, p. 44.
10. A vivid evocation of fashionable women, from an unsigned article, 'Modern Female Dress', in *The Saturday Review*, 2 December 1865, p. 696.
11. John Duguid Milne, *Industrial Employment of Women in the Middle and Lower Ranks*, (revised edition, London, 1870), pp. 74–5.
12. Josephine E. Butler (editor), *Woman's Work and Woman's Culture, A Series of Essays*, (London, 1869), Introduction, p. xxxi.
13. See the unsigned article, 'The Redundancy of Women', *The Saturday Review*, 24 April 1869, pp. 545–6. The arguments reviewed are those of W. R. Greg, put forward in his article 'Why are Women Redundant?' reprinted in his *Literary and Social Judgments*, (London, 1868). He believed that women should be encouraged to emigrate to the United States of America or to the British colonies.
14. Barbara Leigh Smith [afterwards Mme. Bodichon], *Women and Work*, (London, 1857), p. 18.
15. Quoted by Barbara Leigh Smith, op. cit., footnote on pp. 40–41.
16. Munby's diary, Wednesday 17 August 1859. (Munby 2)
17. Mentioned by Lord Houghton at the distribution of prizes to pupils of the Female School of Art, at Burlington House, in 1864; reported under 'Social Science', headed 'Female School of Art', *The Victoria Magazine*, Vol. III (May–Oct. 1864), p. 281.
18. Munby's diary, Tuesday 19 November 1861. (Munby 11)
19. Munby's diary, Sunday 18 February 1866. (Munby 34)
20. The article is signed A.J.M., *Notes and Queries*, 19 February 1881, pp. 144–5.
21. In the 1880s and '90s Munby had an account with Romeike & Curtice, Press Cutting & Information Agency of 359 Strand, who sent him cuttings on women posing as men.
22. This episode, and the details taken from the census are both taken from a lecture given by Emily Faithfull entitled 'Woman's Work, with Special Reference to Industrial Employment'; reproduced in the *Journal of the Society of Arts*, 31 March 1871, p. 382. See also the unsigned article 'The Employment of Females', *Tait's Edinburgh Magazine*, Vol. 27, (1860), pp. 519 and 520.
23. Munby's diary, Saturday 16 May 1863. (Munby 19)
24. Munby's diary, Thursday 9 July 1863. (Munby 19)
25. Munby's diary, Wednesday 29 March 1871. (Munby 39)
26. Munby's diary, Thursday 7 June 1866. (Munby 34)
27. Munby's diary, Friday 22 June, and Friday 6 July 1866. (Munby 34)
28. Munby's diary, Wednesday 7 December 1870. (Munby 38)
29. Munby's diary, Wednesday 22 March 1871. (Munby 39)
30. Munby's diary, Friday 10 April 1863. (Munby 18)
31. From *The 'Girl of the Period' Almanack for 1870* (published in London), headed 'February. – Proposed Post-Office Reform' (the Almanack lacks foliation). It is not known who wrote the 'letters'. The *Almanack* was an offshoot of *The 'Girl of the Period' Miscellany*, published monthly during 1869, to which journalists such as Augustus Mayhew contributed. The phrase had

originated in an unsigned article – which was in fact written by Eliza Lynn Linton – titled 'The Girl of the Period' in *The Saturday Review*, 14 March 1868, pp. 339–40. This was a fairly reactionary piece of journalism along 'young-girls-aren't-what-they-used-to-be' lines, but was interesting in that it sparked off a desultory debate in popular periodicals on the character, behaviour and fashions of modern young women, particularly of the middle classes. *London Society* commented philosophically: 'there have always been girls who liked to do as they pleased, and pleased to do unlike other people, as there are bold spirits in every rising generation who are in advance of their age; and a few of these, who in dress and in manner would have been more pronounced than their neighbours under any conditions.' From an unsigned article entitled 'The Past and Future of the Girl of the Period', *London Society*, Vol. XVI, 1869, p. 466.

4: A Real Social Evil?

Chapter heading quotation: *Report from the Select Committee on Mines* (1866) p. 20; (Minutes of Evidence, questions 650, 651 and 661).

1. Munby's diary, Monday 20 April 1874. (Munby 42)
2. Munby's diary, Thursday 22 September 1864. (Munby 28)
3. John Plummer, *Once a Week*, 27 August 1864, pp. 279 and 280.
4. Emily Faithfull, 'The Unfit Employments in which Women are Engaged', *The Victoria Magazine*, Vol. II (Nov. 1863 – Apr. 1864), p. 71.
5. *First Report of the Children's Employment Commission, on Mines* (1842), p. 76.
6. Ibid., p. 78.
7. Ibid., p. 76.
8. Ibid., p. 47.
9. Marginal annotation in Munby's hand in his copy of the 1842 Report (p. 75), now in the Library of Trinity College, Cambridge.
10. *Children's Employment Commission (1862), Third Report* (published in 1864), p. xxvi.
11. *Children's Employment Commission (1862), Fifth Report* (published in 1866), p. 213. The Coal Mines Regulation Act of 1872 ruled that no women or children could be employed above ground between 9 p.m. and 5 a.m., or after 2 p.m. on Saturday, or on Sunday, thus making such all-night marathons at the pit brow illegal.
12. *Report from the Select Committee on Mines* (1867), p. iii.
13. *Report from the Select Committee on Mines* (1866), pp. 365–6 (Minutes of Evidence, questions 10855 and 10856).
14. Ibid., p. 50 (Minutes of Evidence, questions 1773–5).
15. Ibid., p. 21 (Minutes of Evidence, questions 678–9).
16. Ibid., p. 49 (Minutes of Evidence, question 1745).
17. *Children's Employment Commission (1862), Fifth Report* (published in 1866), p. xvii, note in margin.
18. Elihu Burritt, *Walks in the Black Country and its Green Border-Land*, (London, 1868), pp. 221–3
19. The *Children's Employment Commission (1862), Fifth Report* (published in 1866), p. 152; material contained in a letter concerning 'The Brickyards of South and North Staffordshire, at Jackfield in Shropshire, and other Places', from Francis D. Longe.
20. Ibid., p. xvii.
21. Ibid., p. 127. Evidence given by Mr. Smeed of Sittingbourne, an employer of female brickfield workers, quoted in Mr. H. W. Lord's 'Report on Brickfields'.
22. Munby's diary, Tuesday 4 October 1864. (Munby 28)
23. Munby's diary, Saturday 29 September 1860. (Munby 6)
24. *Report from the Select Committee on Mines* (1867), pp. iv and x.
25. Munby's notebook on his Wigan visit, Friday 17 March 1865. (Munby 97[1])
26. Munby's diary, Friday 14 August 1863. (Munby 20)
27. The *Daily Telegraph*, Tuesday 23 March 1886, p. 5.
28. The *Birmingham Post*, quoted in the *Wigan Observer and District Advertiser*, Friday 26 March 1886, p. 6.
29. The *Pall Mall Gazette*, quoted in the same issue of the *Wigan Observer* etc. as above, p. 6.
30. The *Manchester Guardian*, Wednesday 28 April 1886, p. 8.
31. The *Daily Telegraph*, Monday 22 March 1886, p. 5.
32. The *Daily Telegraph*, Friday 26 March 1886, p. 5.
33. The *Wigan Observer* etc., Saturday 10 April 1886, p. 7. The Rev. Harry Mitchell was speaking at a meeting of pit brow women at Westleigh, about five miles from Wigan, and six miles from his parish of Pemberton.
34. From a letter signed A.J.M. in the *Wigan Observer* etc., Saturday 30 January 1886, p. 2.
35. *The Times*, Tuesday 11 May 1886, p. 6. This letter was timed to coincide with the introduction of the Mines Regulation Bill for its second reading in Parliament.
36. The *Daily Telegraph*, Monday 22 March 1886, p. 5.
37. The Rev. Harry Mitchell, reported in the *Daily Telegraph*, Monday 22 March 1886, p. 5.
38. The *Birmingham Post*, quoted in the *Wigan Observer* etc., Friday 26 March 1886, p. 6.
39. *The Times*, Wednesday 18 May 1887, p. 11.

5: 'Honest labour bears a lovely face'

Chapter heading quotations:
   from Munby's notebook (Munby 97[2])
   from *The Photographic News*, 18 Oct. 1861, p. 500; quoted by Helmut and Alison Gernsheim in *The History of Photography, from the camera obscura to the beginning of the modern era*, (revised edition, London 1969), p. 239.

1. Quoted by Daniel J. Boorstin in *The Image*, Pelican Books, (Harmondsworth, 1963), p. 19.
2. In 1864 Robert Cecil commented in *The Quarterly Review*: 'Photographers of the economical class are rather in the habit of using lenses for taking cartes de visite which are not made to cover easily quite the whole of the plate they employ. The result is, that the feet of the standing figure are apt to be involved in the margin of hazy distortion that marks the limit at which the clearness of the lens begins to fail.' From 'Photography', loc. cit., Vol. 116, p. 512.

3. Gernsheim, op. cit., p. 301.

4. John A. Randall, 'A History of Photographic Prices', *The British Journal of Photography*, 25 June 1897, p. 410.

5. Elizabeth, Lady Eastlake, 'Photography' in *The Quarterly Review*, Vol. 101, (1857), p. 443.

6. Unsigned article, 'A Photographer's Story', *Sharpe's London Magazine*, Vol. XIX, 1861, p. 36.

7. Mrs. Hoare, a rag cutter interviewed by Mr. H. W. Lord; published in the evidence in the *Fourth Report of the Children's Employment Commission (1862)*, published in 1865.

8. Elizabeth, Lady Eastlake, op. cit., p. 465.

9. Munby's diary, Saturday 27 July 1861. (Munby 9)

10. Mayhew had recorded 'a photographic Man' as saying 'When we are not busy, we always fill up the time taking specimens for the window.' (*London Labour and the London Poor*, Vol. III; London, 1861; p. 208). It seems likely that some of Munby's photographs – especially the London ambrotypes – were such specimens.

11. Munby's diary, Wednesday 16 October 1861: (Munby 11)

12. Munby's diary, Friday 24 January 1862. (Munby 12)

13. Munby's diary, Saturday 1 March 1862. (Munby 12)

14. Hannah Cullwick, 'A servant's life 1866 to 1872', p. 77. (Munby 98[17])

15. Ibid., p. 43.

16. Munby's diary, Saturday 1 March 1862. (Munby 12)

17. Munby's diary, Wednesday 13 April 1859. (Munby 1)

18. Munby's diary, Thursday 19 May 1859. (Munby 1)

19. Munby's diary, Friday 18 March 1864. (Munby 24)

20. Munby's diary, Tuesday 28 February 1860. (Munby 4)

21. Munby's diary, Saturday 11 May 1867. (Munby 35)

22. This can be compared with another photograph by Rejlander entitled *The Chimney Sweep* (c. 1862–8), in which the sweep is posed with his brushes on the same studio stairs. For a reproduction see Edgar Yoxall Jones, *Father of Art Photography: O. G. Rejlander 1813–1875*, (Newton Abbot, 1973), p. 94.

23. Hannah's diary, Sunday 28 April 1872. (Munby 98[6])

24. Photography's supposed truthfulness and exact rendering imposed upon the noun 'photograph' a new meaning – an accurate description. It appears with this meaning in the titles of books which were *not* illustrated with photographs, such as *Midnight Scenes and Social Photographs, being descriptions of the street wynds and dens of the city*, by "Shadow" (Glasgow, 1858), and E. C. Grenville Murray, *Under the Lens: Social Photographs*, (London, 1885).

25. Samuel Bourne, 'Photography in the East', *The British Journal of Photography*, 1 July 1863, p. 268.

26. Elizabeth Gaskell, *North and South*, Penguin edition, (Harmondsworth, 1970), p. 448.

27. Norman McCord in his article 'Photographs as historical evidence' has been able, thanks to the local knowledge of the mining historian Steve Martin, to identify all but one of the men in this photograph: 'the top-hatted figure on extreme left is Mr Humble, manager of the disaster pit. Next to him, in sinkers' typical working kit, are the Coulsons, father and son, two of the leaders among the pit-sinking experts of the area. When the disaster occurred they were working on sinking a shaft at West Sleekburn, having just completed work at North Seaton in 1861. They were at once called away to rescue operations at Hartley. The top-hatted man, centre, is Charles Carr, owner of the stricken New Hartley pit, and a leading figure in local mining management. An unidentified sinker stands at Carr's left and at extreme right is David Wilkinson, another well known local sinker, and the first man through the Hartley debris in 1862 to find that there were no survivors.' *The Local Historian*, February 1978, Vol. 13, No. 1, p. 35.

28. *Samuel Johnson, Selected Writings*, Penguin edition, (Harmondsworth, 1968), p. 331. Samuel Johnson's *A Journey to the Western Isles of Scotland*, was first published in 1775; the journey took place in 1773.

29. Munby's diary, Thursday 20 August 1863. (Munby 21)

30. Munby's diary, Monday 9 November 1863. (Munby 31)

31. For other examples of his work and an account of the background to it, see Andrew Lanyon, *The Rooks of Trelawne*, (London, 1976).

32. Munby's diary, Tuesday 9 February 1864. (Munby 23)

33. Munby's diary, Tuesday 2 June 1874. (Munby 42)

34. Munby's diary, Monday 24 March 1862. (Munby 12)

35. Munby's diary, Saturday 28 May 1864. (Munby 25)

36. Munby's diary, Saturday 22 March 1862. (Munby 12)

37. Munby's diary, Friday 23 May 1862. (Munby 13).
The 'photographic man' interviewed by Mayhew had told him: 'Sunday is the best day for shilling portraits; in fact, the majority is shilling ones, because then, you see, people have got their wages, and don't mind spending. Nobody knows about men's ways better than we do. Sunday and Monday is the Derby-day, like, and then after that they are about cracked up and done. The largest amount I've taken at Southwark on a Sunday is 80 – over 4l. worth, but then in the week-days it's different; Sunday's 15s. we think that very tidy, some days only 3s. or 4s.' *London Labour and the London Poor*, Vol. III, (London, 1861), p. 207.

38. From the column 'Miscellanea', paragraph headed 'Indecent Photographs: Severe Sentence', in *The British Journal of Photography*, 25 March 1870. Henry Evans was evidently not a major dealer in 'photographic studies from life'. When the premises of Henry Hayler, a Pimlico photographer, were raided in 1874, 130,248 obscene photographs and 5,000 obscene stereoscopic slides were seized. Hayler had already fled to the Continent. (See *The Times*, 20 April 1874).

39. Munby's diary, Saturday 24 January 1863. (Munby 17)

40. Munby's diary, Friday 20 February 1863. (Munby 17)

II: PORTRAITS FROM LIFE

These extracts are taken from Munby's diaries and notebooks. The spelling and punctuation are his. I have inserted the occasional quotation mark where Munby failed to notice his omission in the course of his several revisions of his diaries – these he dated at the back of each volume. I have also written out in full the word 'and' where Munby uses & or, more often, ∝.

After 1864 Munby used commercially printed diaries instead of pocketbooks with blank pages. As might have been expected, he was unable to contain his enthusiasms within the space allotted for each day and wrote in a tiny script which sometimes shrank to thirteen or fourteen lines of handwriting to the inch – considerably smaller than the 'small print' of newspapers. When cramped for space he sometimes used abbreviations which in ordinary circumstances he would have written out in full. I have taken the liberty of doing this for him in the hope that I am making his entries clear without changing their meaning. Thus where he writes: 'Went down by steep trod, found A.B.', I have expanded it to read: 'I went down by the steep trod, and found Annie Born'. This has only been necessary for a few entries. Otherwise I have let Munby speak for himself, although as the length of his diary entries sometimes reached several thousand words *per day*, it should always be borne in mind that a great deal has had to be omitted for reasons of space.

Under each section heading will be found the source of the extracts and details of other material I have used, following the sequence in the text.

Wigan Pit Brow Girls

Section heading quotation: Munby's diary, Friday 29 September 1871. (Munby 39)
Munby's diary, Friday 19 August 1859. (Munby 3)
Munby's diary, Saturday 29 September 1860. (Munby 6)
Munby's diary, Tuesday 18 August 1863.
        Wednesday 19. (both Munby 20)
Munby's Wigan notebook, Friday 17 March 1865. (Munby 97[1])
Munby's Wigan notebook, Monday 10 September 1866.
        Tuesday 11. (both Munby 97[3])
Munby's diary, Wednesday 10 September 1873.
        Thursday 11. (both Munby 41)
Munby's Wigan notebook, Monday 14 September 1874. (Munby 97[6])
Munby's Wigan notebook, Wednesday 18 September 1878. (Munby 97[7])

South Wales Mine Tip Girls

Munby's diary, Sunday 10 October 1869. (Munby 37)
Munby's notebook, Friday 22 September 1865. (Munby 97[2])

Women Miners in Belgium

Munby's diary, Monday 1 September 1862. (Munby 15)
1. Louis Simonin, *La Vie souterraine, ou les mines et les mineurs* (1867); the English edition was entitled *Underground Life; or, Mines and Miners*, trans. adapted and ed. H. W. Bristow, (London, 1869), p. 241.
2. Werner Thönnessen, *The Emancipation of Women; the Rise and Decline of the Women's Movement in German Social Democracy 1863–1933*, trans. Joris de Bres, (Pluto Press, 1973; originally published: Frankfurt am Main, 1969), p. 43.
3. See 'Exposition de 1861. Rapport du Jury etc.', *Bulletin Belge de la Photographie*, Tome premier, (1862), p. 13. Their report read: 'M. Bevière [sic], de Charleroi, nous a montré des *Ouvriers houilleurs au travail*: ils sont bien groupés et les types sont originaux;

l'execution photographique est très-bonne; malheureusement, il a pointillé et retouché beaucoup de ses figures; il a eu tort, surtout pour celles du deuxième plan qui étaient suffisamment nettes sans ce travail.'
4. Émile Zola, *Germinal*, trans. Leonard Tancock, Penguin Books, (Harmondsworth, 1954), pp. 31 and 134. It is interesting to read in Zola's working notes his early idea to centre the strike in *Germinal* around the issue of the mining company wishing to throw the women out of the pits. See Émile Zola, *Mes Notes sur Anzin*, Bibliothèque Nationale, Paris; MS 10.308, feuillet 222.
5. Unsigned article entitled 'Pit Brows and Piano Legs', *The Saturday Review*, 21 May 1887, p. 715.

Fishergirls of the Yorkshire Coast

Munby's diary, Monday 31 October 1864. (Munby 28)
Munby's diary, Tuesday 14 February 1865.
        Tuesday 21.
        Thursday 9 March. (all Munby 33)
1. Munby's notebook. Undated note headed 'Filey fishwomen & girls'. The entry was almost certainly made in 1865. (Munby 97[1])
2. Munby's diary, Tuesday 7 March 1865. (Munby 33)
3. Munby's diary, Friday 10 February 1865. (Munby 33)
4. Munby's notebook, Tuesday 24 January 1865. (Munby 97[1])
Munby's diary, Tuesday 15 October 1867.
        Wednesday 16. (both Munby 35)
Munby's diary, Thursday 15 October 1868. (Munby 36)
Munby's diary, Thursday 30 December 1869. (Munby 37)
Munby's diary, Saturday 30 December 1893. (Munby 60)

London Milkwomen

Munby's diary, Saturday 20 July 1861. (Munby 9)
1. Described by Munby in his diary, Friday 30 January 1863, (Munby 17) and Tuesday 28 April 1863, (Munby 18). For an attack on the image of the 'simple milkmaid', see 'The Milkwoman', by James Greenwood – 'The Amateur Casual' – in *London Society*, Vol. XXII, 1872, pp. 529–35. For the adulteration and pollution of milk see the unsigned article 'Milk and Coals' in *The Saturday Review*, 11 October 1873, pp. 459–60, and the unsigned article 'Death in the Milk Can', in *The Saturday Review*, 23 August 1873, pp. 237–8.
Munby's diary, Saturday 11 June 1864. (Munby 25)
Munby's diary, Thursday 27 July 1865. (Munby 33)
Munby's diary, Thursday 1 February 1872. (Munby 40)

Female Gymnasts

Munby's diary, Thursday 14 August 1862. (Munby 14)
Munby's diary, Monday 7 September 1868. (Munby 36)
Munby's diary, Saturday 11 June 1870. (Munby 38)
Munby's diary, Monday 6 February 1871. (Munby 39)

Maids-of-all-Work

Section heading quotation: from 'Duties of the Maid-of-all-Work' in *Beeton's Book of Household Management*, edited by Mrs. Isabella

Beeton, (London, 1861), p. 1001.

Hannah's diary, Tuesday 30 September 1873. (Munby 98[7])

Hannah's diary, Wednesday 23 December 1863.

   Thursday 24.

   Friday 25.

   Saturday 26. (all Munby 98[1])

1. This extract does not refer directly to domestic servants. It comes from an unusual article which describes the daily battle for survival of the poor in London and makes biting comments by describing human beings as extraordinarily resilient machines. Unsigned article, 'London Shadows, No. 1 – Bread made out of River Drift', *London Society*, Vol. VII, 1865, p. 347.

Hannah's diary, Sunday 1 January 1871. (Munby 98[5])

2. 1871 was the year that one of Munby's best friends and a colleague both at Trinity College, Cambridge and at the Ecclesiastical Commissioners', R. B. Litchfield, married, and Munby lamented the loss of 'the last but one of my unmarried friends'. Two years later he was to marry Hannah, the servant who washed in a bucket. The gulf which divided Mrs. Litchfield – Henrietta, daughter of Charles Darwin – from the future Mrs. Munby, and, indeed, the gulf which separated mistresses from their servants generally, can be appreciated in this account of Mrs. Litchfield – Aunt Etty – by her niece Gwen Raverat:

   'I have defined Ladies as people who did not do things themselves. Aunt Etty was most emphatically such a person. She told me, when she was eighty-six, that she had never made a pot of tea in her life; and that she had never in all her days been out in the dark alone, not even in a cab; and I don't believe she had ever travelled by train without a maid. She certainly always took her maid with her when she went in a fly to the dentist's. She asked me once to give her a bit of the dark meat of a chicken, because she had never tasted anything but the breast. I am sure that she had never sewn on a button, and I should guess that she had hardly ever even posted a letter herself. There were always people to do these things for her. In fact, in some ways, she was very like a royal person. Once she wrote when her maid, the patient and faithful Janet, was away for a day or two: "*I am very busy answering my own bell.*" And I can well believe it, for Janet's work was no sinecure. But, of course, while Janet was away, the housemaid was doing all the real work; and Aunt Etty was only perhaps finding the postage stamps for herself, or putting on her own shawl – the sort of things she rang for Janet to do, every five minutes all day long.'

   from *Period Piece, A Cambridge Childhood*, by Gwen Raverat, new ed. (London, 1960), pp. 119–20.

Hannah's diary, Wednesday 10 May 1871. (Munby 98[5])

Hannah's diary, Friday 12 May 1871. (Munby 98[5])

Hannah's diary, Thursday 15 June 1871 (Munby 98[5])

Hannah's diary, Tuesday 25 July 1871. (Munby 98[5])

3. Munby recording a story told by Hannah 'about ladies, from a servant's point of view', 'Hannah 1885 and Cary Juliet – Visits to Hannah Vol. 1'. (Munby 66)

Hannah's diary, Sunday 22 January 1871. (Munby 98[5])

Hannah's diary, Tuesday 30 September 1873. (Munby 98[7])

III 'WOMAN'S RIGHTS'

This poem was first published in Arthur Munby's *Poems New and Old*, (London, 1865), III, pp. 87–104.

Index